SCOTT FORESMAN · ADDISON WESLEY

Mathematics

Grade 3

Reteaching Masters/Workbook

PEARSON

Scott Foresman

Editorial Offices: Glenview, Illinois • Parsippany, New Jersey • New York, New York

Sales Offices: Parsippany, New Jersey • Duluth, Georgia • Glenview, Illinois
Coppell, Texas • Ontario, California • Mesa, Arizona

Overview

Reteaching Masters/Workbook provides additional teaching options for teachers to use with students who have not yet mastered key skills and concepts covered in the student edition. A pictorial model is provided when appropriate, followed by worked-out examples and a few partially worked-out exercises. These exercises match or are similar to the simpler exercises in the student edition.

ISBN 0-328-04967-0

4 5 6 7 8 9 10 V084 09 08 07 06 05 04

Name_____

Ways to Use Numbers

Numbers can be used to locate, to name, to measure, and to count.

Locate

Name

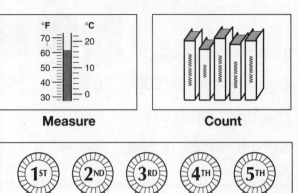
Measure

Count

Numbers can also be used to show the order of people or objects. These are called ordinal numbers.

1ST 2ND 3RD 4TH 5TH

Tell if each number is used to locate, name, measure, or count.

1.

2.
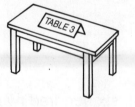

3.
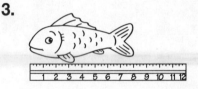

_____   _____   _____

Use the picture below for 4–7.

Striped   Dotted   Gray   Starred   White

4. Which ball is third in line?   _____

5. Write an ordinal number for the white ball's
place in line.   _____

6. Which ball is second in line?   _____

7. Which ball is fourth in line?   _____

8. Number Sense What ordinal number would come
next in the following list? 10th, 11th, 12th, . . .   _____

Numbers in the Hundreds

Here are different ways to show 612.

place-value blocks:

expanded form: 600 + 10 + 2

standard form: 612

word form: six hundred twelve

Write each number in standard form.

1.

_____

2.

_____

3. 400 + 30 + 7   **4.** six hundred twenty   **5.** 200 + 50 + 1

_____   _____   _____

6. three hundred forty-five   _____

Write the word form for each number.

7. 285   _____

8. 892   _____

9. 146   _____

10. 378   _____

11. **Number Sense** Write a three-digit number with a
2 in the hundreds place and a 4 in the tens place.   _____

Name_____

Place-Value Patterns

Here are three different ways to show 114.

114 = 1 hundred, 1 ten, 4 ones

114 = 11 tens, 4 ones

114 = 1 hundred, 14 ones

Use place-value blocks to show 140 in two ways. Draw the blocks you use for each answer.

1. Using only hundreds and tens blocks

2. Using only tens blocks

Write each number in standard form.

3.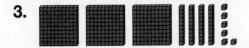

4.

_____   _____

5. Writing in Math Can you draw 321 using only place-value blocks for hundreds and tens? Explain.

_____

_____

Name_____

Numbers in the Thousands

Here are different ways to show 2,263.

place-value blocks:

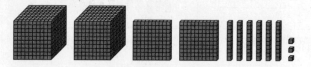

expanded form: 2,000 + 200 + 60 + 3

standard form: 2,263

word form: two thousand, two hundred sixty-three

Write each number in standard form.

1.

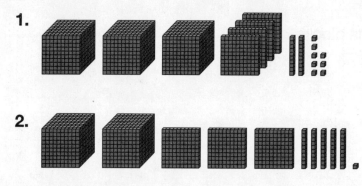

_____

2.

_____

3. 7,000 + 400 + 40 + 8   _____

4. five thousand, seven hundred fifty-five   _____

Write each number in expanded form.

5. 1,240   _____

6. 6,381   _____

7. Number Sense Write a four-digit number with a
7 in the thousands place and a 6 in the ones place. _____

8. Reasoning Jason will build a number with the digits 4, 7, 2,
and 6. In what order should he put the digits if he
wants to make the greatest number possible? _____

Name_____

Greater Numbers

A period is a group of three digits in a number, starting from the right. A comma is used to separate two periods.

Thousands Period			Ones Period		
hundred thousands	ten thousands	thousands	hundreds	tens	ones
2	4	7 ,	3	6	2

Here are different ways to show 247,362.

expanded form: 200,000 + 40,000 + 7,000 + 300 + 60 + 2

standard form: 247,362

word form: two hundred forty-seven thousand, three hundred sixty-two

Write each number in standard form.

1. 60,000 + 8,000 + 200 + 50 + 1 _____

2. 30,000 + 600 + 30 + 2 _____

3. four hundred one thousand, four hundred fifty-four _____

4. five hundred twenty-nine thousand, three hundred seventy-eight _____

5. Write 522,438 in expanded form.

_____

6. Write 349,281 in expanded form.

_____

7. **Number Sense** What is the value of the 7 in 86,752? _____

8. Lake Erie is 32,630 square miles. Write the area of Lake Erie in expanded form.

_____

PROBLEM-SOLVING SKILL

Read and Understand Problems

School Bus Routes Tim's bus travels 5 miles from his house to school. Ann's bus travels 8 miles from her house to school. How many miles do the two buses travel together?

> **Read and Understand**

Step 1: What do you know?

- Tell the problem in your own words.

  Each school bus travels a number of miles.

- Identify key facts and details.

  Tim's bus travels 5 mi. Ann's bus travels 8 mi.

Step 2: What are you trying to find?

- Tell what the question is asking.

  We want to know total miles both buses travel.

- Show the main idea.

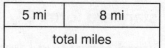

5 mi	8 mi
total miles	

Use addition to find the answer. 5 + 8 = 13 mi

Sharing Marbles Jamal had a bag of marbles. He gave 6 red marbles and 3 green marbles to Josh. How many marbles did Jamal give to Josh?

1. Identify key facts and details. _____

_____

2. Tell what the question is asking. _____

_____

4. Show the main idea. Use it to solve the problem.

5. Write your answer in a complete sentence.

_____

_____

Comparing Numbers

When you compare numbers, you use these symbols.

< is less than   **> is greater than**   **= is equal to**

You can compare numbers using place-value blocks, a number line, or by comparing digits that are in the same place.
Compare 375 and 353.

   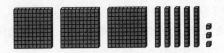

Both have the same number of hundreds.

375 has more tens, so 375 > 353, or 353 < 375.

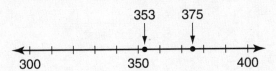

375 is to the right of 353, so 375 > 353. 353 is to the left of
375, so 353 < 375, or 353 is less than 375. Both have the same
number of hundreds. Seven tens is greater than five tens.
So, 375 > 353, or 353 < 375.

3 7 5
↑ ↑
↓ ↓
3 5 3

Compare the numbers. Use <, >, or =. Use any method.

1. 5 ◯ 3

2. 39 ◯ 93

3. 1,025 ◯ 1,025

4. 842 ◯ 824

5. 3,121 ◯ 1,099

6. 12,492 ◯ 10,863

7. Writing in Math Every digit in 8,999 is greater than any
digit in 24,005. Explain why 24,005 is greater than 8,999.

_____

_____

_____

Ordering Numbers

To order numbers from greatest to least or least to greatest, you can use a number line.

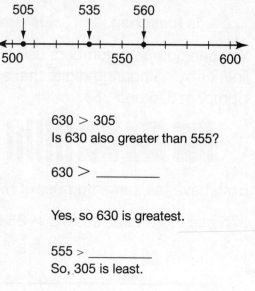

These numbers, in order from least to greatest, are 505, 535, and 560.

You can also use place value to order numbers. First, you compare pairs of numbers to find the greatest number. Then you compare the other numbers.

630 > 305

Is 630 also greater than 555?

630 > _____

Yes, so 630 is greatest.

555 > _____

So, 305 is least.

National Monument	Total Height
Statue of Liberty	305 ft
Washington Monument	555 ft
Gateway Arch	630 ft

Write the numbers in order from least to greatest.

```
←——+——+——+——+——+——+——+——+——+——+——→
   550  555  560  565  570  575  580  585  590  595  600
```

1. 560 583 552   _____

2. 583 575 590   _____

3. 576 580 557   _____

Write the numbers in order from greatest to least.

4. 973 1,007 996   _____

5. 5,626 5,636 5,616   _____

6. 445 455 450   _____

7. Representations Jamie is 9 years old, Al is 12 years old, David is 3 years old, and Naomi is 6 years old. Draw a number line from 1 to 12. Put these ages on the number line from least to greatest.

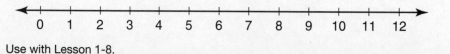

Number Patterns

You can use a number line to find a number pattern.

Find the pattern. Find the next two numbers.

17, 14, 11, 8, _____ , _____

A hundred chart can help you find
39 − 12 using place-value patterns.
Start at 39 and move up one row
to subtract 10. Then move two columns
to the left to subtract 2 ones.
39 − 12 = 27.

1	2	3	4	5	6	7	8	9	10
11	12	13	14	15	16	17	18	19	20
21	22	23	24	25	26	27	28	29	30
31	32	33	34	35	36	37	38	39	40
41	42	43	44	45	46	47	48	49	50
51	52	53	54	55	56	57	58	59	60

Continue each pattern.

1. 4, 8, 12, ☐ , ☐

2. 90, 80, 70, ☐ , ☐

3. 7, 14, 21, ☐ , ☐

4. 25, 50, 75, ☐ , ☐

Use place-value patterns to find each sum or difference.

5. 18 + 20

6. 21 + 17

7. 46 − 12

_____ _____ _____

8. **Writing in Math** Explain how you can use a hundred chart
   to subtract 12 from 46.

_____

_____

_____

_____

Rounding Numbers

You can use place value to round to the nearest ten or hundred.

Find the rounding place. If the digit in the ones or the tens place is 5, 6, 7, 8, or 9, then round to the next greater number. If the digit is less than 5, do not change the digit in the rounding place.

Round 17 to the nearest ten: _20_____

Explain. _7 is in the ones place. Round to the next greater ten._

Round 153 to the nearest ten. _150_____

Explain. _Because 3 is in the ones place and 3 is less than 5, the digit in the tens place doesn't change._

Round 1,575 to the nearest hundred. _1,600_____

Explain. _Because the 7 in the tens place is 5 or greater, round to the next greater hundred._

---

1. Round 63 to the nearest ten: _____

   Explain. _____

Round each number to the nearest ten.

2. 58   3. 71   4. 927   5. 3,121

_____   _____   _____   _____

Round each number to the nearest hundred.

6. 577   7. 820   8. 2,345   9. 8,750

_____   _____   _____   _____

10. **Reasoning** If you live 71 mi from a river, does it make sense to say you live about 80 mi from the river? Explain.

_____

Plan and Solve

Hurdle Jumping Rashid and Juan set up a 50 m hurdle race.
They set one hurdle at 5 m, one at 45 m, and one at every 5 m
in between. How many hurdles will the runners cross?

Step 1: Choose a strategy.	Step 2: Stuck? Don't give up. Try these.
• **Show what you know:** Draw a picture, make an organized list, make a table or graph, use objects/act it out.	• Reread the problem.
	• Tell the problem in your own words.
• **Look for a Pattern**	• Tell what you know.
• **Try, Check, and Revise**	• Identify key facts and details.
• **Use Logical Reasoning**	• Show the main idea.
• **Solve a Simpler Problem**	• Try a different strategy.
• **Work Backward**	• Retrace your steps.
• **Write a Number Sentence**	**Step 3: Answer the question in the problem.**

What strategy can be used? Drawing a picture will help solve this problem.

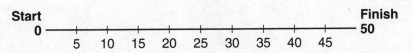

The answer to the problem: The runners will cross 9 hurdles.

Beaded Bracelets Sue is able to make six beaded bracelets
each month. If Sue begins on January 1st, how many bracelets
will she be able to finish in time for the crafts sale on May 2nd?

1. What strategy might work to solve this problem?

   _____

   _____

2. Give the answer to the problem in a complete sentence.

   _____

   _____

Counting Money

You can count on to find the value of coins and bills. When you count money, start with the bills, then follow with the coins of greatest value. This is what you say when you count on to get to $7.52.

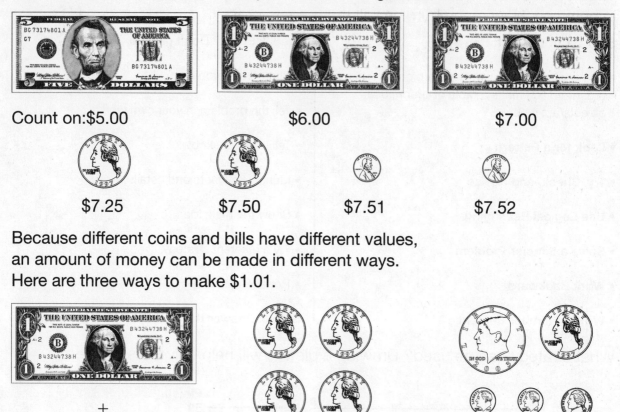

Count on:$5.00 $6.00 $7.00

$7.25 $7.50 $7.51 $7.52

Because different coins and bills have different values, an amount of money can be made in different ways. Here are three ways to make $1.01.

+

Write the total value in dollars and cents.

1.

_____

2. What bills and coins could you use to show $8.60?

_____

_____

Making Change

Suppose you bought a sandwich that costs $3.75 and gave the clerk a $5 bill. The clerk might first say "$3.75." Then he or she might hand you a quarter and say "$4.00," then hand you a dollar and say "$5.00." The clerk counted on from the price of your item to the amount you paid with to find your change.

$3.75 $4.00 $5.00

Your change would be $1.25.

Use the School Cafeteria menu to the right. List the coins and bills you would use to make change. Then write the change in dollars and cents.

School Cafeteria Menu	
Daily Special	$3.49
Fruit Cup	$1.95
Salad	$2.09
Corn Muffin	$1.50
Milk	$0.75

1. Emilio bought a corn muffin with two $1 bills.

    _____

    _____

2. Marco bought a Daily Special with a $5 bill.

    _____

    _____

3. **Number Sense** Craig bought a milk with a $1 bill. Write two different ways he could receive his change.

    _____

    _____

4. **Reasoning** Andrea bought a salad and a milk. She got a dime, a nickel, a penny, and two $1 bills in change. How much did Andrea give the clerk? _____

Name_____

Look Back and Check

Planting Flowers Max had 120 bulbs to plant in the fall. There were 48 daffodil bulbs, and the rest were tulip bulbs. How many tulip bulbs did Max have to plant?

You are not finished with the problem until you look back and check your answer.

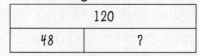

Paige's Work

120	
48	?

120 – 48 = 72
Max planted 72 tulip bulbs.

Step 1: Check your answer.
Did Paige answer the right question?
Yes, she found the number of tulip bulbs Max planted.

Step 2: Check your work.
Paige could use place-value patterns to check if her answer is correct.
She can use a number line to skip count by 10s.

Did Paige use the correct operation?
Paige used subtraction to find the number of tulip bulbs Max planted.

Camera Sales A camera company wants to sell at least 130 cameras each week. One week they sold 38 cameras with zoom lenses and 86 regular cameras. Did they sell at least 130 cameras that week?

Martin's Work

$$38 \quad\quad\quad\quad\quad 86$$
$$\downarrow \quad\quad\quad\quad\quad\quad \downarrow$$

30 40 50 60 70 80 90

I know that 38 can be rounded to 40 and 86 can be rounded to 90.

40 + 90 = 130; Yes. The camera store sold enough cameras.

1. Did Martin answer the right question? Explain.

_____

_____

_____

2. Is his work correct? Explain.

_____

_____

_____

Name _____

White-Tailed Deer

White-tailed deer that live in the desert weigh less than their eastern relatives. The average weight of an adult male Desert White-tailed deer is about 200 pounds. The females have an average weight of about 125 pounds. Use place value to compare.

200
↑
↓   2 hundreds is greater than
     1 hundred.
125

You could say 200 > 125, or 125 < 200.

So, the male white-tailed deer weighs more than the female white-tailed deer.

White-tailed deer can run as fast as 40 miles per hour. Suppose the speed of one deer is recorded at 37 miles per hour. The speed of another deer is recorded at 23 miles per hour.

1. Compare the speeds of the two deer, using the > and < symbols.

   _____

2. How much faster did the first deer run than the second deer? Show your work and write your answer in a complete sentence.

   _____

   _____

   _____

3. Nena paid $4.75 to hike in a state park for one day. She paid with a $20 bill. How much change did she receive?

   _____

Addition Properties

The Commutative (order) Property

You can add numbers in any order, and the sum will be the same.

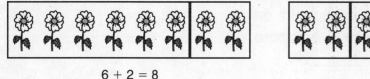

6 + 2 = 8   2 + 6 = 8

The Associative (grouping) Property

You can group addends in any way, and the sum will be the same.

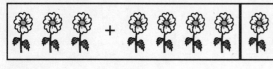

(3 + 4) + 1 = 8   3 + (4 + 1) = 8

The Identity (zero) Property

The sum of any number and zero equals that same number.

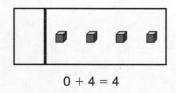

0 + 4 = 4

Find each sum.

1. $3 + (2 + 4) =$ _____   **2.** $(0 + 5) + 2 =$ _____

3. $(8 + 3) + 4 =$ _____   **4.** $9 + 2 + 6 =$ _____

Write each missing number.

5. $3 + 4 = 4 +$ _____   **6.** _____ $+ 7 = 7$

7. $(2 + 3) + 4 =$ _____ $+ (2 + 4)$ **8.** $9 + (2 + 7) = (9 + 2) +$ _____

9. Reasoning Does $(4 + 5) + 2 = 9 + 2$? Explain.

_____

_____

Relating Addition and Subtraction

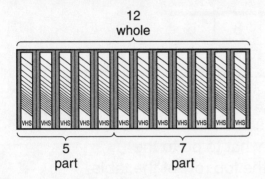

12
whole

5
part

7
part

When you know the parts and the whole, you can write a fact family. Here is a fact family that uses the numbers 5, 7, and 12.

$5 + 7 = 12$ $12 - 5 = 7$

$7 + 5 = 12$ $12 - 7 = 5$

Complete each fact family.

1. $3 + 5 =$ _____ $8 -$ _____ $= 3$

_____ $+ 3 = 8$ _____ $- 3 = 5$

2. $9 + 2 =$ _____ $11 -$ _____ $= 9$

_____ $+ 9 = 11$ _____ $- 9 = 2$

Find each missing number.

3. $7 +$ _____ $= 14$ **4.** _____ $+ 5 = 11$

5. $4 +$ _____ $= 12$ **6.** $6 +$ _____ $= 15$

7. Number Sense Write a subtraction fact using 6 such as
$6 - \blacksquare = \blacksquare$. Then write an addition fact you could use to check it.

_____

_____

_____

Find a Rule

In	1	3	2	4	8	6
Out	0	2	1	3	7	

Each number in the top row, **In,** of the table is related to the number in the bottom row, **Out,** by the same rule. The rule in this table is **subtract 1.** A rule explains what to do to the numbers that you put **In,** like those on the top row of the table, to get the numbers that come **Out.**

Complete the table.

1.

In	4	3	1	5	2	7
Out	7	6	4	8		

2. Write the rule, such as **subtract 1.** _____

Complete each table. Then write a rule for the table.

3.

In	5	20	15	10	30
Out	10	25	20		

Rule: _____

4.

In	16	17	10	13	11
Out	9	10	3		

Rule: _____

5. Writing in Math The rule is **add 4.** Make your own table with an In and Out pattern to match the rule.

Name_____

Write a Number Sentence

Suppose you do two tasks today. How much money would you earn if you walked the dog and made your bed?

Task	Pay
Walk Dog	$2.00
Do Dishes	$1.25
Make Bed	$1.00

To write a number sentence to solve a problem, follow these four steps:

Step 1: Show the main idea.

n	
$2.00	$1.00

Step 2: Decide which operation fits the main idea.

You must add to find the missing sum.

Step 3: Use a letter to show what you are trying to find.

Step 4: Solve the number sentence.

The n shows how much money you will make.

$2 + $1 = n
You will make $3.

Finally, look back and check your answer. Is your answer reasonable? $2 + $1 = $3. Yes, it is reasonable.

Use the task price list. Write a number sentence with a variable. Then solve.

1. Tommy did the dishes and made his bed. How much money did Tommy earn?

_____

2. Alice gets $5 allowance each week. Her parents take away money from her allowance if she does not do tasks. This week Alice forgot to make her bed twice. How much allowance will Alice get this week?

_____

3. **Writing in Math** Write a word problem using the task price list. Then solve your problem. Explain how you know your answer is correct.

_____

Name _____

Mental Math:
Break Apart Numbers

You can break apart numbers to make them easier to add mentally.

Find 31 + 45 using mental math.
There are two ways.

First, break apart the numbers into tens and ones.   **or**   Break apart only one number.

	tens		ones
31 =	30	+	1
45 =	40	+	5

Add the tens together: 30 + 40 = 70.

Add the ones together: 1 + 5 = 6.

Finally, add the tens and the ones together: 70 + 6 = 76.

So, 31 + 45 = 76.

45 = 40 + 5

Then add 40 + 31 = 71.

Next add the 5 to 71:

71 + 5 = 76

So, 31 + 45 = 76.

Find each sum using mental math.

1. 52 + 12 = _____   **2.** 24 + 71 = _____   **3.** 36 + 43 = _____

4. 47 + 50 = _____   **5.** 54 + 23 = _____   **6.** 24 + 72 = _____

7. 33 + 46 = _____   **8.** 22 + 64 = _____   **9.** 34 + 53 = _____

10. Number Sense To add 32 + 56, Juanita first added
32 + 50. What numbers should she add next?   _____

11. In June, 46 cars were sold. There were 12 cars sold in April.
How many more cars were sold in June than in April?

_____

Name_____

Mental Math: Using Tens to Add

To add mentally, you can break numbers apart to make a ten.

For example, to find 26 + 17, you can break the numbers apart like this:

A.

26 + 17

B. You can break 17 into 4 + 13.

4 + 13

C. Add 26 + 4 = 30.

26 + 4 = 30

D. Then add 30 + 13 = 43.

30 + 13 = 43

So, 26 + 17 = 43.

To find 46 + 9, you could first find 46 + 10 = 56. Then you can subtract 1 from the answer. 56 − 1 = 55. This is the same sum as 46 + 9.

Find each sum using mental math.

1. 67 + 9 = _____ **2.** 35 + 8 = _____ **3.** 46 + 7 = _____

4. 25 + 49 = _____ **5.** 37 + 56 = _____ **6.** 87 + 13 = _____

7. Reasonableness Marcie says, "To find 87 + 7, I can find 87 + 10 and then subtract 3." Do you agree? Explain?

_____

_____

_____

_____

Estimating Sums

Suppose your class is saving 275 cereal box tops for a fundraising project. Your class has 138 Fruity Cereal box tops and 152 Bran Cereal box tops. Does your class have enough box tops for the project? Since you only need to know if you have enough, you can estimate.

Here are some ways you can estimate.

Rounding: Round each addend to the nearest hundred or to the nearest ten. Then add and compare.

Round to the nearest *hundred*.	Round to the nearest *ten*.
$152 \Rightarrow 200$	$152 \Rightarrow 150$
$+138 \Rightarrow 100$	$+138 \Rightarrow 140$
$= 300$	$= 290$
Since $300 > 275$, you have enough.	Since $290 > 275$, you have enough.

Front-end estimation: Use the front digit of each number and zeroes for the rest.

$152 \Rightarrow 100$
$+138 \Rightarrow 100$
$= 200 < 275$

Compatible numbers: Use numbers that are close but easy to add.

$152 \Rightarrow 150$
$+138 \Rightarrow 140$
$= 290 > 275$

Round to the nearest ten to estimate each sum.

1. $37 + 117$ _____

2. $42 + 98$ _____

Round to the nearest hundred to estimate each sum.

3. $240 + 109$ _____

4. $87 + 588$ _____

5. Reasonableness Sun-Yi estimated $270 + 146$ and got 300. Is this reasonable? Explain.

_____

_____

_____

Name_____

Overestimates and Underestimates

R 2-8

Overestimate: An overestimate happens when you round up.

Gina has 36 tomato plants and 57 pepper plants. If she has 100 pots, does she have enough for the plants? Round to the nearest ten to estimate the sum.

36 rounds up to 40
+ 57 rounds up to _60_
100   She has enough pots.

Each addend was rounded *up* so the estimated sum is *greater than* the actual sum. It is an overestimate.

Underestimates: An underestimate happens when you round down.

Gerry is in charge of seating for the school show. She has set up 34 seats in the center and 23 seats on each side. She is expecting 70 people. Has she set up enough chairs? Round to the nearest ten to estimate the sum.

34 rounds down to 30
23 rounds down to 20
+ 23 rounds down to _20_
70 seats is the estimated sum.

Each addend was rounded *down*, so the estimated sum, 70, is *less than* the actual sum. It is an underestimate.

Estimate each sum by rounding to the nearest ten. Then tell whether each estimate is an overestimate or an underestimate.

1. 36 + 47 _____

2. 11 + 44 _____

3. Number Sense Liz wants to send two packages. The shipping cost for one package will be $42, and the other will cost $38. Liz has $100. Estimate the total cost of shipping the packages. Does Liz have enough money? Explain.

_____

_____

Name _____

Mental Math: Using Tens to Subtract

You can change numbers to tens to make subtraction problems easier.

There are two ways we can subtract 42 − 28.

One way to make this problem simpler is to change 28 to 30, because it is easier to subtract 30 from 42.

Then, add 2 to the answer because you subtracted 2 too many.
$42 - 28 = (42 - 30) + 2 = 14$

Another way is to add the same amount to each number.

$$42 \quad - \quad 28$$

$$\Downarrow \qquad \Downarrow$$

$$+2 \quad +2$$

$$\Downarrow \qquad \Downarrow$$

$$44 - 30 = 14$$

So, $42 - 28 = 14$.

Find each difference using mental math.

1. $32 - 17 = $ _____ **2.** $51 - 46 = $ _____ **3.** $42 - 17 = $ _____

4. $29 - 17 = $ _____ **5.** $63 - 56 = $ _____ **6.** $78 - 19 = $ _____

7. $94 - 18 = $ _____ **8.** $55 - 33 = $ _____ **9.** $87 - 24 = $ _____

10. Number Sense To solve $39 - 27$, Anika changed it to $(40 - 27) + 1$. Is this a simpler problem? Explain.

_____

_____

_____

Mental Math: Counting On to Subtract

Erica wanted to find a new way to subtract mentally. She wondered if counting on would help her to subtract. When you count on, you change a subtraction problem into an addition problem that is missing an addend.

Erica thought that to find $86 - 47$, she would change the problem into $47 + \blacksquare = 86$.

First, she would count by ones up to the nearest ten: $47 + 3 = 50$.

Then, she would count by tens up to 80: $50 + 30 = 80$.

Then she counted up to 86: $80 + 6 = 86$.

Finally Erica added all the numbers she counted up by: $3 + 30 + 6 = 39$.

So, $86 - 47 = 39$.

Count on to find each difference mentally.

1. $60 - 32 =$ _____   **2.** $48 - 12 =$ _____   **3.** $53 - 17 =$ _____

4. $69 - 24 =$ _____   **5.** $76 - 37 =$ _____   **6.** $42 - 28 =$ _____

7. $96 - 85 =$ _____   **8.** $56 - 28 =$ _____   **9.** $84 - 69 =$ _____

Algebra Count on to find the value of the missing number.

10. $37 +$ _____ $= 59$ **11.** $76 +$ _____ $= 90$ **12.** $48 +$ _____ $= 65$

13. Number Sense Rob wants to spend $60 on birthday presents for Samir. Rob buys Samir a hat that costs $37. How much money does Rob have left to buy Samir another birthday present? Write the number sentence you would use to solve the problem. Then solve.

Estimating Differences

Members of the Biology Club caught 136 grasshoppers and 188 butterflies in nets. How many more butterflies than grasshoppers did the club catch?

Here are four different ways to estimate differences.

Round to the nearest hundred:

    188 rounds to 200
 − 136 rounds to 100

About 100 more butterflies than grasshoppers

Round to the nearest ten:

    188 rounds to 190
 − 136 rounds to 140

About 50 more butterflies than grasshoppers

Use compatible numbers:

    188 is close to 185
 − 136 is close to 135

About 50 more butterflies than grasshoppers

Use front-end estimation:

    188 ⇒ 100
 − 136 ⇒ 100

About the same number of butterflies and grasshoppers

Use any method to estimate each difference.

1. 68 − 42 _____

2. 88 − 17 _____

3. 442 − 112 _____

4. 346 − 119 _____

5. 692 − 87 _____

6. 231 − 109 _____

7. Writing in Math Chuck estimated 287 − 29 and got a difference of about 200. Is this a reasonable estimate? Explain.

_____

_____

_____

_____

_____

Name_____

You can explain your answer to a problem by breaking the problem into steps. For example:

If you wanted to go on the pony ride and the Ferris wheel, would you need more than 40 tickets?

Carnival Ride Costs

Ferris Wheel	23 tickets
Pony Ride	24 tickets
Water Slide	18 tickets
Moonwalk	12 tickets

Ask yourself if an exact answer or an estimate is needed.

The problem asks if you need more than 40 tickets. An exact answer is not needed. An estimate is enough.

Then, decide which operation you should use and why.

To solve this problem, you should add because you are putting together the number of tickets needed.

Finally, find the answer and explain how you found it.

Step 1: Round 24 down to 20

Step 2: Round 23 down to 20

Step 3: 20 + 20 = 40

Step 4: Both numbers were rounded down, so more than 40 tickets are needed.

1. Joe wants to go on the water slide and the pony ride. How many tickets will he need? Explain how he can find the exact number of tickets using mental math.

_____

_____

2. Renaldo read a book that has 286 pages. Roz read 179 pages of a different book. About how many more pages did Renaldo read than Roz? Show the problem you used to find the answer.

_____

PROBLEM-SOLVING APPLICATIONS
Big Cats

The tiger is the largest animal in the cat family and the only cat that consistently has stripes.

There used to be 8 kinds of tigers. Three of the kinds have become extinct, or disappeared.

How many kinds of tigers are left?

You can subtract to find the answer.

$8 - 3 = 5$

So, there are 5 kinds of tigers left.

Suppose a tiger eats 33 lb of meat one night and 39 lb of meat on another night.

1. Round 33 and 39 to the nearest tens place. _____

2. Find the sum of the rounded numbers. _____

3. How many pounds of meat did the tiger eat in the two nights? Show your work and write your answer in a complete sentence.

_____

_____

Suppose Country A has 288 tigers in zoos and Country B has 171 tigers in zoos. How many more tigers does Country A have than Country B?

4. Find an estimate by rounding each number to the nearest ten. _____

5. Find the actual difference. Write your answer in a complete sentence.

_____

_____

Adding Two-Digit Numbers

To find 27 + 57, first estimate. 27 is close to 30. 57 is close to 60. 30 + 60 = 90, so the answer should be about 90.

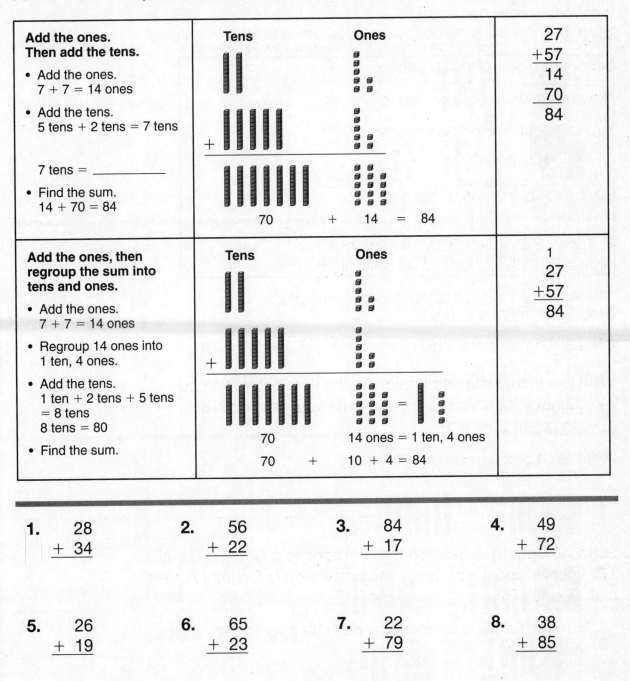

Add the ones.
Then add the tens.
 	
• Add the ones.
  7 + 7 = 14 ones
 	
• Add the tens.
  5 tens + 2 tens = 7 tens
 	
  7 tens = _____
 	
• Find the sum.
  14 + 70 = 84
	Tens Ones
	
	70 + 14 = 84
		27
		+57
		14
		70
		84

Add the ones, then
regroup the sum into
tens and ones.
 	
• Add the ones.
  7 + 7 = 14 ones
 	
• Regroup 14 ones into
  1 ten, 4 ones.
 	
• Add the tens.
  1 ten + 2 tens + 5 tens
  = 8 tens
  8 tens = 80
 	
• Find the sum.
	Tens Ones
	
	70 14 ones = 1 ten, 4 ones
	70 + 10 + 4 = 84
		1
		27
		+57
		84

1.   28
 + 34

2.   56
 + 22

3.   84
 + 17

4.   49
 + 72

5.   26
 + 19

6.   65
 + 23

7.   22
 + 79

8.   38
 + 85

9. **Reasonableness** Hannah added 65 and 26 and got 81.
   Is this answer reasonable? Explain.

Models for Adding Three-Digit Numbers

Find 152 + 329.

Step 1: Show each number with place-value blocks.

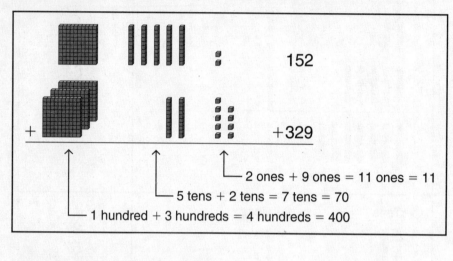

$$2 \text{ ones} + 9 \text{ ones} = 11 \text{ ones} = 11$$
$$5 \text{ tens} + 2 \text{ tens} = 7 \text{ tens} = 70$$
$$1 \text{ hundred} + 3 \text{ hundreds} = 4 \text{ hundreds} = 400$$

Step 2: Combine the ones. $2 + 9 = 11$

Step 3: Combine the tens. $50 + 20 = 70$

Step 4: Combine the hundreds. $100 + 300 = 400$

Step 5: Add. $400 + 70 + 11 = 481$

Write each problem and find the sum.

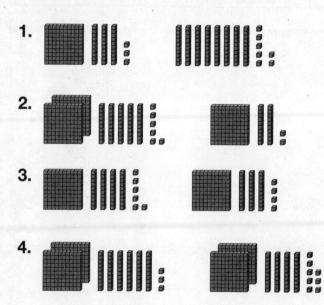

1. _____

2. _____

3. _____

4. _____

Adding Three-Digit Numbers

Find 237 + 186.

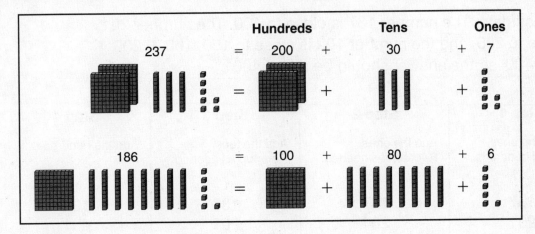

Step 1: Add the ones. 7 ones + 6 ones = 13 ones

Regroup. 13 ones = 1 ten, 3 ones

Step 2: Add the tens. 1 ten + 3 tens + 8 tens = 12 tens

Regroup. 12 tens = 1 hundred, 2 tens

Step 3: Add the hundreds.

1 hundred + 2 hundreds + 1 hundred = 4 hundreds

Add together the hundreds, tens, and ones.

400 + 20 + 3 = 423

---

1. 118 + 146	**2.** 283 + 147	**3.** 542 + 109	**4.** 220 + 479

5. Find the sum of 456 and 38. _____

6. Add 109 and 656. _____

7. Estimation Estimate to decide which sum is
less than 600: 356 + 292 or 214 + 356. _____

Name_____

Adding Three or More Numbers

Find 137 + 201 + 109.

First, estimate. The number 137 is close to 100. The number 201
is close to 200, and the number 109 is close to 100. 100 + 200 +
100 = 400, so the answer should be about 400.

Step 1	Step 2	Step 3	Step 4
Line up the ones, tens, and hundreds.	Add the ones. Regroup as needed.	Add the tens. Regroup as needed.	Add the hundreds.
137 201 + 109	1 137 201 + 109 7	1 137 201 + 109 47	1 137 201 + 109 447
All the numbers are in neat columns so you can add them easily.	Regroup 17 ones into 1 ten and 7 ones.	No need to regroup.	So, 137 + 201 + 109 = 447.

Check to see if the answer is reasonable. Your estimate was
400. 447 is close to 400, so the answer is reasonable.

1.   32
        64
      + 71

2.   127
        39
      + 87

3.   17
        68
      + 32

4.   358
       427
      + 27

5. 382 + 45 + 181 = _____

6. 12 + 138 + 98 = _____

7. **Number Sense** Ranier has 37 baseball cards, 65 football
    cards, and 151 hockey cards. How many sports cards
    does he have in all?

    _____

Name_____

PROBLEM-SOLVING STRATEGY

Draw a Picture

R 3-5

Fruit Stand Don is selling 18 watermelons. If he sold 7 watermelons in the morning and 6 more during the early afternoon, how many more watermelons could he still sell by the end of the day?

Read and Understand

Step 1: What do you know?

Don is selling 18 watermelons. He has sold 7 in the morning and 6 in the afternoon.

Step 2: What are you trying to find?

How many watermelons Don can still sell by the end of the day

Plan and Solve

What strategy will you use?

Strategy: Draw a picture.

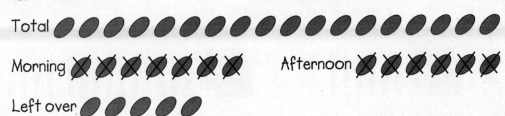

Answer: Don can still sell 5 more watermelons by the end of the day.

Look Back and Check

Is your answer reasonable?

I can see from the picture that $7 + 6 + 5 = 18$.

Draw a picture to help you solve the problem, then write the answer.

1. Mike, Bob, and John each gave a balloon to each of the others in the group. How many balloons were given in all?

Name_____

Regrouping

You can regroup from tens to ones and hundreds to tens by using place-value blocks.

1 ten can be regrouped into 10 ones.

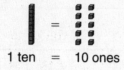

1 ten = 10 ones

1 hundred can be regrouped into 10 tens.

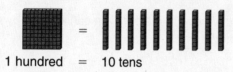

1 hundred = 10 tens

Place-value blocks can also help you to regroup numbers containing hundreds or tens into numbers with tens and ones.

1 hundred gets regrouped into 10 tens.

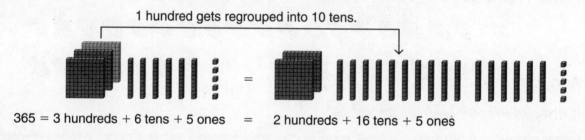

365 = 3 hundreds + 6 tens + 5 ones = 2 hundreds + 16 tens + 5 ones

Regroup 1 ten for 10 ones. You may use place-value blocks or draw a picture to help.

1. 32 = 3 _____ tens 2 _____ ones   2. 47 = 4 _____ tens 7 _____ ones

Regroup 1 hundred for 10 tens. You may use place-value blocks or draw a picture to help.

3. 176 = 1 _____ hundred 7 _____ tens 6 ones

4. 243 = 2 _____ hundred 4 _____ tens 3 ones

5. **Number Sense** Explain why 249 = 1 hundred, 14 tens, 9 ones.

_____

_____

Subtracting Two-Digit Numbers

Here is how to subtract two-digit numbers.

Find 55 − 36.

Estimate: 60 − 40 = 20, so the answer should be about 20.

What You Think	What You Show		What You Write
Step 1 Subtract the ones. Regroup if you need to. Since you can't subtract 6 from 5, regroup.		Regroup 1 ten into 10 ones. 15 ones − 6 ones = 9 ones.	4 15 5̸5̸ −36 9
Step 2 Subtract the tens.		4 tens − 3 tens = 1 ten.	4 15 5̸5̸ −36 19

Add to check your answer. 19 + 36 = 55

It checks.

---

1.   86
        − 51

2.   47
        − 18

3.   62
        − 35

4.   41
        − 11

5. 28 − 17 _____

6. 53 − 38 _____

7. Number Sense To subtract 91 from 99, do you need to regroup? Explain.

_____

_____

8. Felicia has 67 paperback books in her collection. She sold 48 of them. How many books does she have left? _____

Models for Subtracting Three-Digit Numbers

You can use place-value blocks to subtract.

Find 234 − 192.

Estimate: 230 − 190 = 40, so the answer should be about 40.

	What You Show	**What You Write**
Step 1 Show 234 with place-value blocks.		234 −192
Step 2 Subtract the ones. Regroup if needed. 4 > 2. No regrouping is needed.	4 ones − 2 ones = 2 ones	234 −192 2
Step 3 Subtract the tens. Regroup if needed. 3 tens < 9 tens, so regroup 1 hundred for 10 tens.	13 tens − 9 tens = 4 tens	1 13 234 −192 42
Step 4 Subtract the hundreds.	1 hundred − 1 hundred = 0 hundreds	1 13 234 −192 42

Find the value of the remaining blocks:

4 tens + 2 ones = 40 + 2 = 42

So, 234 − 192 = 42.

Find each difference. You may use place-value blocks or draw a picture to help.

1. 156
− 28

2. 191
− 122

3. 321
− 76

4. 446
− 355

Name_____

Subtracting Three-Digit Numbers

Find 726 − 238.

Estimate: 700 − 200 = 500, so the answer should be about 500.

Step 1	**Step 2**	**Step 3**
First subtract the ones. Regroup if needed.	Subtract the tens. Regroup if needed.	Subtract the hundreds.
1 16 72̶6̶ −238 — 8	11 6 1̶ 16 7̶2̶6̶ −238 — 88	11 6 1̶ 16 7̶2̶6̶ −238 — 488
Regroup 1 ten into 10 ones.	You will need to regroup, since 3 tens > 1 ten. Regroup 1 hundred into 10 tens. This gives you a total of 11 tens.	Is your answer correct? Check by adding: 488 + 238 = 726. It checks.

1. 228
    − 123

2. 291
    − 187

3. 336
    − 275

4. 512
    − 299

5. 175 − 156 = _____

6. 327 − 159 = _____

7. The town library had 634 CDs for rent. During one week, 288 of them were rented. How many CDs were left?

_____

8. **Number Sense** If you had to subtract 426 from 913, how many times would you need to regroup? How can you tell?

_____

_____

_____

_____

Subtracting Across Zero

To subtract from a number with a zero in the tens place, you need to first regroup a hundred into tens.

Find 207 − 98.

Step 1	Step 2	Step 3
Subtract the ones. Regroup if necessary.	Regroup the hundreds.	Regroup the tens and subtract.

Step 1:
$$\begin{array}{r} 207 \\ -\ 98 \\ \hline \end{array}$$

Normally you would regroup 1 ten into 10 ones. Since there are no tens, you must first regroup hundreds.

Step 2:
$$\begin{array}{r} {}^{1\ 10} \\ 2\cancel{0}7 \\ -\ 98 \\ \hline \end{array}$$

2 hundreds and 0 tens is equal to 1 hundred and 10 tens. Now you can regroup the tens.

Step 3:
$$\begin{array}{r} {}^{9\ 17} \\ {}^{1\ \cancel{10}} \\ 2\cancel{0}\cancel{7} \\ -\ 98 \\ \hline 109 \end{array}$$

10 tens and 7 ones is the same as 9 tens and 17 ones. Now you can subtract.

1.
$$\begin{array}{r} 302 \\ -\ 72 \\ \hline \end{array}$$

2.
$$\begin{array}{r} 105 \\ -\ 36 \\ \hline \end{array}$$

3.
$$\begin{array}{r} 300 \\ -\ 228 \\ \hline \end{array}$$

4.
$$\begin{array}{r} 500 \\ -\ 223 \\ \hline \end{array}$$

5. 105 − 37 = _____

6. 301 − 192 = _____

7. Dave and Chris went bowling. Dave knocked down 300 pins and Chris knocked down 187 pins. How many fewer pins did Chris knock down than Dave? _____

8. Writing in Math Use place-value blocks to draw a picture showing one way to find 406 − 202.

Name_____

Exact Answer or Estimate?

There are times when an estimate is enough to solve a problem. Sometimes an exact answer is needed.

Reading Competition Sanjay and Teresa are having a reading competition. The table shows how many books each has read. How many more books has Sanjay read than Teresa?

Month	Sanjay	Teresa
January	12 books	15 books
February	27 books	21 books
March	22 books	8 books
April	6 books	13 books

The problem asks for an exact answer. To find out the exact answer, you need to add the books read by Sanjay and the books read by Teresa. Sanjay read 67 books. Teresa read 57 books. Then you need to subtract the number of books read by Teresa from the number of books read by Sanjay. $67 - 57 = 10$. Sanjay read exactly 10 more books than Teresa.

If the question had been "Who has read more books, Sanjay or Teresa?" an estimate would be enough.

Water Park Crowd On a sunny day, 108 people were at the water park. After an hour, 36 people had left. A little bit later, 24 people came back to the water park. How many people are now at the water park?

1. What operations will you use? Explain.

   _____

   _____

2. Is an estimate enough? Explain.

   _____

   _____

3. Solve the problem. Write your answer in a complete sentence.

   _____

   _____

Name_____

Adding and Subtracting Money

Find $12.50 + $9.25.

Estimate: $13 + $9 = $22.

Step 1	**Step 2**
Add as you would with whole numbers. Make sure to line up the decimal points before adding.	Write the answer in dollars and cents. Be sure to include the decimal point.

Step 1:
```
    1
  $12.50
+    9.25
   21 75
```

Step 2:
```
    1
  $12.50
+    9.25
  $21.75
```

$12.50 + $9.25 = $21.75

---

1. $2.87
    + 1.09

2. $15.31
    − 2.27

3. $ 3.67
    + 13.22

4. $10.07
    − 0.88

5. $7.65 + $0.82 _____

6. $17.21 − $12.33 _____

7. $14.31 + $36.29 _____

8. $9.27 − $8.85 _____

9. Wallace bought a model airplane for $6.93.
   He paid with a $20 bill. How much change did
   Wallace get back?   _____

10. **Writing in Math** Samina wants to pay for some balloons
    with a $10 bill. The balloons cost $1.79. Samina estimates
    that she will get $7.00 back in change. Do you agree with
    her estimate? Explain.

    _____

    _____

    _____

Choose a Computation Method

Use mental math to solve problems that are simple.

Example: 250 + 200

Use paper and pencil, and make estimates to solve problems
with two or more regroupings.

Example: 524 + 217
I estimate 524 to be 500. I estimate 217
to be 200. So, my answer should be about 700.
My estimate of 700 is close to 741.

$$\begin{array}{r} 1 \\ 524 \\ +\ 217 \\ \hline 741 \end{array}$$

Use a calculator to solve problems with many regroupings.
Example: 23,142 − 17,565
First I'll estimate by rounding to the nearest thousand:
23,000 − 18,000 = 6,000.
23,142 − 17,565 = 5,577

My estimate of 6,000 is close to 5,577.

Use mental math, paper and pencil, or a calculator to solve.

1.	2.	3.	4.
1,200 + 800	$26.91 + 42.03	300 − 109	96,346 − 18,982

5. Backbone Mountain in Maryland is 3,360 ft high. Mount
Washington in New Hampshire is 6,288 ft high. How much
higher is Mount Washington than Backbone Mountain?
Write your answer in a complete sentence.

_____

_____

_____

_____

Name_____

Equality and Inequality

A number sentence that uses < (less than) or > (greater than) is an inequality. Example: 8 > 1 + 6. This equation is read as 8 is *greater than* 1 + 6.

You can add or subtract on each side of a number sentence to decide if the sentence is true or false.

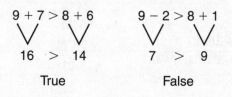

$$9 + 7 > 8 + 6$$

16 > 14

True

$$9 - 2 > 8 + 1$$

7 > 9

False

Find a number to make the number sentence true.

3 + _____ > 8

Try 2.   3 + 2 > 8

           5 > 8 False

Try 7.   3 + 7 > 8

           10 > 8 True

Compare. Write <, >, or = for each $\bigcirc$.

1. 13 + 7 $\bigcirc$ 20

2. 14 + 22 $\bigcirc$ 37 + 1

3. 42 − 18 $\bigcirc$ 27 + 6

4. 28 − 14 $\bigcirc$ 5 + 9

Find three whole numbers that make each number sentence true.

5. 5 + _____ < 15

_____

6. 19 − _____ < 12

_____

7. 27 + _____ > 30

_____

Name_____

Small Countries

This chart shows the area of several small countries.

If Grenada's area was increased by 84 square kilometers, how many square kilometers would it be?

Land Areas

Country	Area (square kilometers)
Monaco	2
Nauru	21
San Marino	60
Marshall Islands	181
Maldives	300
Malta	321
Grenada	339

Step 1	**Step 2**	**Step 3**
Add the ones. Regroup. 13 ones = 1 ten, 3 ones	Add the tens. Regroup. 12 tens = 1 hundred, 2 tens	Add the hundreds.

Step 1:
```
  1
 339
+ 84
   3
```

Step 2:
```
 1 1
 339
+ 84
  23
```

Step 3:
```
 1 1
 339
+ 84
 423
```

$339 + 84 = 423$

Grenada would be 423 square kilometers.

---

1. What is the area of Nauru and San Marino combined? _____

2. What is the area of the Marshall Islands and Maldives combined? _____

3. How much larger is Malta than Nauru? _____

4. How much smaller is San Marino than Grenada? _____

5. What is the area of Malta, Maldives, and the Marshall Islands combined? _____

Time to the Half Hour and Quarter Hour

Time can be measured in half hours and quarter hours.

30 minutes = 1 half hour

15 minutes = 1 quarter hour

The hours of a day are divided into A.M. and P.M. hours. A.M. hours begin at 12 midnight and end at 12 noon. P.M. hours begin at 12 noon and end at 12 midnight.

The clocks show the times of three events that happen every day at an elementary school.

Reading	Lunch	Recess

What you write: 9:30   12:15

Here are different ways to say each time.

    9:30   **nine thirty** or **half past nine**

    12:15   **twelve fifteen** or **fifteen minutes after twelve** or **quarter after twelve**

    1:45   **one forty-five** or **fifteen minutes to two** or **quarter to two**

Write the time shown on each clock in two ways.

1.   7:15   _____

_____

2.   _____

_____

Time to the Minute

You can skip count by fives and then count on to tell time when the minute hand is between numbers.

The minute hand is between 7 and 8.

Count by 5s from 12 to 7. That is 35 minutes.

Count 3 more minutes. There are 38 minutes.

The hour hand is between 11 and 12. The time is 11:38, or 22 minutes to 12.

Write the time shown on each clock two ways.

1. _____
_____
_____

2. _____
_____

3. _____

Elapsed Time

A children's museum is open from 1:00 P.M. to 6:35 P.M. every day. How long is the museum open?

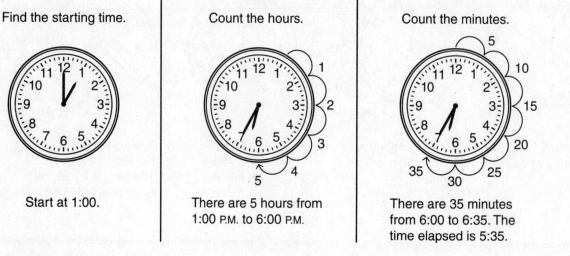

Step 1	**Step 2**	**Step 3**
Find the starting time.	Count the hours.	Count the minutes.
Start at 1:00.	There are 5 hours from 1:00 P.M. to 6:00 P.M.	There are 35 minutes from 6:00 to 6:35. The time elapsed is 5:35.

Find the elapsed time.

1. **Start time:** 8:00 A.M.
   End time: 1:15 P.M. _____

2. **Start time:** 3:25 A.M.
   End time: 5:40 A.M. _____

3. **Start time:** 12:00 P.M.
   End time: 3:48 P.M. _____

4. **Number Sense** A science class lasted from 1:15 until 2:05. Did the science class last more than or less than 1 hr?

   _____

Name_____

Using a Calendar

You can use a calendar to find the days of the week and the months of a year.

Time	Order of the Months
1 week = 7 days	January
	February
52 weeks = 1 year	March
	April
1 year = 12 months	May
	June
1 year = 365 days	July
	August
1 leap year = 366 days	September
	October
1 decade = 10 years	November
	December
1 century = 100 years	

November						
S	M	T	W	T	F	S
						1
2	3	4	5	6	7	8
9	10	11	12	13	14	15
16	17	18	19	20	21	22
23	24	25	26	27	28	29
30						

What is the ninth month of the year?

> Count nine months starting with January. September is the ninth month of the year.

What date is the second Tuesday in November?

> Locate the Tuesday column on the calendar. The 4th is the first Tuesday, and the 11th is the second Tuesday.

---

1. How many Mondays were there in November? _____

2. What date was the fourth Friday in November? _____

3. How many Sundays were there in November? _____

4. What day of the week was November 12? _____

5. **Number Sense** About how many days are there in two months?

_____

6. Write the ordinal number that represents the month of November when the months of the year are listed in order. _____

7. **Number Sense** How many weeks are in two years? _____

Use with Lesson 4-4. **47**

Using Tally Charts to Organize Data

Students were asked, "What is your favorite subject at school?" You can use tally charts to help you organize data you collect from the survey.

Each subject that students chose as their favorite was listed, and a tally mark was recorded for each time that subject was given as an answer.

Period	Tally Marks	Number
Reading	卌 ‖	7
Math	卌 卌 │	11
Science	‖‖	4
Gym	卌 │	6

1. What is the most popular subject in the survey? _____

2. How many students answered the survey altogether? _____

3. In the survey, what is the least popular subject? _____

4. **Number Sense** What number is shown by

   卌 卌 ‖‖ _____

Use the data at the right for 5–7.

5. Make a tally chart to show the results.

Favorite Animal			
Lion	Duck	Lion	Tiger
Bear	Tiger	Bear	Lion
Bear	Lion	Tiger	Tiger
Tiger	Lion	Duck	Bear

6. How many people voted? _____

7. Which animals got the same number of votes?

_____

Using Line Plots to Organize Data

This line plot shows the size in centimeters of a group of caterpillars. Each X represents one caterpillar.

Caterpillar Length

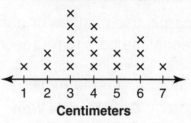

To find the range of this set of data, you subtract the least number from the greatest number. $7 - 1 = 6$, so the range of the data is 6.

To find the mode of this set of data, you look to see which centimeter measure appears most often on the line plot. Three centimeters has the most Xs above it, so the mode of the data is 3 cm.

A group of third graders sold tomato plants to help buy a new flagpole for the school. The number of tomato plants students sold is shown on the line plot. Use the line plot to answer 1–6. Each X represents one student.

Number of Plants Sold

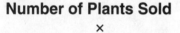
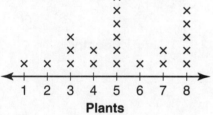

1. What is the mode of this data? _____

2. How many students sold exactly five plants each? _____

3. How many students sold exactly six plants? _____

4. How many students sold fewer than five plants each? _____

5. What is the range of this data? _____

6. **Reasoning** Two students sold exactly the same number of plants. How many could they have sold? List all of the possible answers. _____

Name_____

Reading Pictographs and Bar Graphs

Pictographs use pictures or parts of pictures to represent data.
Bar graphs use bars to represent data.

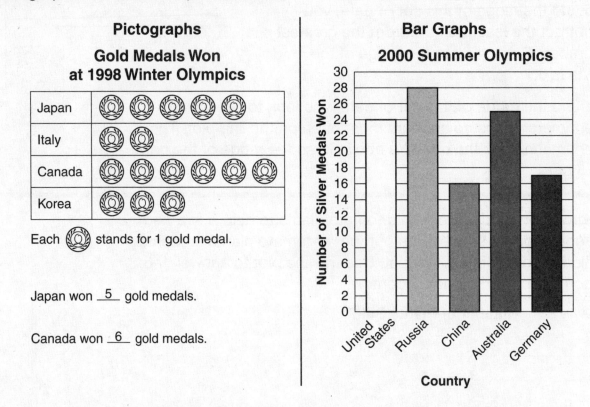

Pictographs

Gold Medals Won at 1998 Winter Olympics

Each stands for 1 gold medal.

Japan won _5_ gold medals.

Canada won _6_ gold medals.

Bar Graphs

2000 Summer Olympics

_____ won 28 silver medals in 2000.

Germany won _____ silver medals in 2000.

1. How many houses were built in City B in 2002?

_____

2. How many houses were built in City A in 2002?

_____

Number of Houses Built in 2002

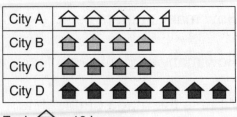

Each 🏠 = 10 houses.
Each 🏠 = 5 houses.

Name_____

PROBLEM-SOLVING SKILL R 4-8

Writing to Compare

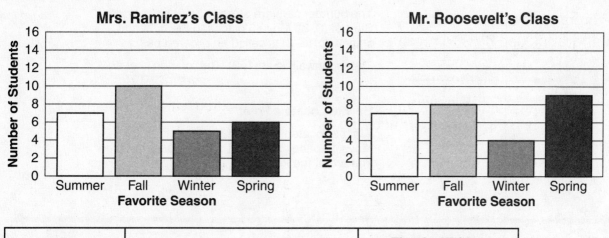

Question	Comparison Statements	Tips for Writing Good Comparisons
How are the groups alike?	Winter is the least favorite season for both groups. Summer had the same number of votes for both groups.	Use comparison words such as *most*, *least*, and *about the same*.
How are the groups different?	Fall had the greatest number of votes in Mrs. Ramirez's class, but spring had the greatest number of votes in Mr. Roosevelt's class.	Use contrast words such as *but* or *however*.

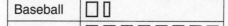

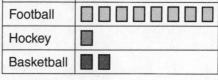

Bill's Sports Card Collections

Baseball	▢
Football	▨▨▨▨▨
Hockey	▨▨▨▨▋
Basketball	▨▨▨▨▨

Each ▢ = 10 cards.

Terry's Sports Card Collections

Baseball	▢▯
Football	▨▨▨▨▨▨▨
Hockey	▨
Basketball	▨▨

Each ▢ = 10 cards.

1. Write a statement about how Bill and Terry's collections are alike.

_____

_____

2. Write a statement about how Bill and Terry's collections are different.

_____

Use with Lesson 4-8. **51**

Graphing Ordered Pairs

The Amusement Park

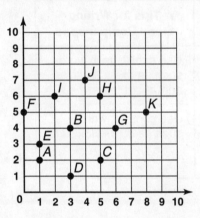

How to Name a Point

The bumper cars are at point (3, 2) on the grid. Start at (0, 0). Move 3 places to the right and 2 places up. (3, 2) is called an ordered pair.

The moonwalk is at (1, 3). The log ride is at (2, 4).

How to Locate a Point

What is located at (1, 1)?
Move 1 space to the right and 1 space up.
You are at the food court. It is at (1, 1).

Write the ordered pair that describes the location of each point.

1. A _____

2. B _____

3. C _____

4. D _____

Give the letter of the point named by each ordered pair.

5. (0, 5) _____

6. (8, 5) _____

7. (1, 3) _____

8. (6, 4) _____

9. Writing in Math Describe the difference between locating a point at (1, 3) and a point at (3, 1).

_____

_____

Name_____

Reading Line Graphs

How can you find out how much rain fell at 1 P.M. on Monday?

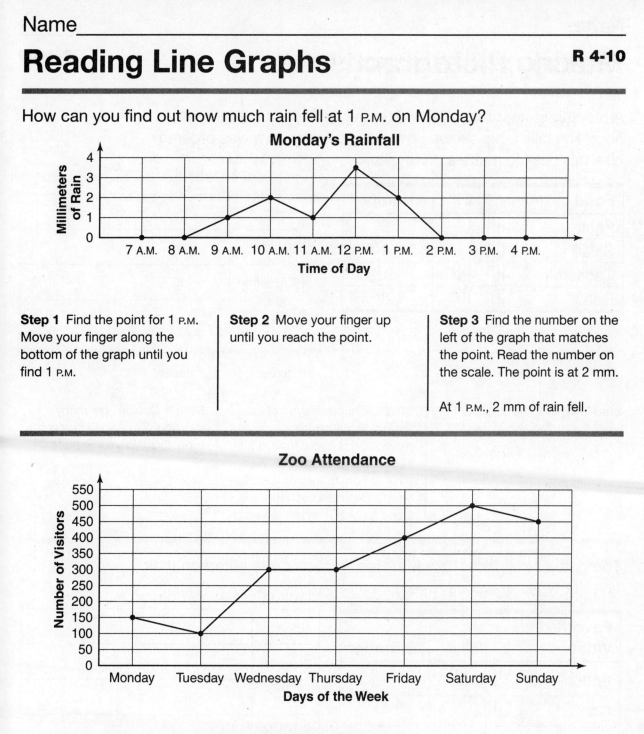

Monday's Rainfall

Step 1 Find the point for 1 P.M. Move your finger along the bottom of the graph until you find 1 P.M.

Step 2 Move your finger up until you reach the point.

Step 3 Find the number on the left of the graph that matches the point. Read the number on the scale. The point is at 2 mm.

At 1 P.M., 2 mm of rain fell.

Zoo Attendance

1. How many people visited the zoo on Monday? _____

2. How many days did less than 350 people visit the zoo? _____

3. **Reasoning** Is it correct to say that the zoo was the most crowded on the weekend? Explain.

_____

_____

Name_____

Making Pictographs

A restaurant kept track of the number of items it sold in one hour. The tally table shows how many of each item was ordered. Use this data to make a pictograph.

Food	Tally	Number
Pasta	ＨＨ Ｉ	6
Salad	ＩＩＩＩ	4
Casserole	ＨＨ ＨＨ	10
Fish	ＨＨ ＩＩＩ	8

Pasta	
Salad	
Casserole	
Fish	

Each ___ = ___ meals.

Step 1 Write a title to explain what the pictograph shows.

Step 2 Choose a symbol for the key. Because this pictograph is about food, a fork might be a good symbol. Add your symbol to the key. Decide how many votes each fork will stand for. Add this to the key.

Step 3 Decide how many symbols are needed for each food. Draw them.

The data below show how Ms. Hashimoto's class voted on their favorite types of videos to rent.

Favorite Video	Tally	Number
Action	ＨＨ ＩＩＩ	
Comedy	ＩＩＩ	
Drama	ＨＨ Ｉ	
Animated	ＨＨ ＨＨ	

Action	
Comedy	
Drama	
Animated	

Each 📼 = ___ votes.

1. Complete the table.

2. Complete the pictograph.

3. **Writing in Math** Write a title for the table and pictograph above.

_____

Name_____

Making Bar Graphs

The table shows the number of different kinds of birds that visited a bird feeder over five days.

Day	Number of Birds
Monday	6
Tuesday	4
Wednesday	7
Thursday	5
Friday	3

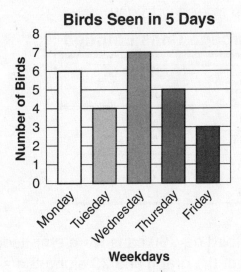

Birds Seen in 5 Days

How to make a bar graph:

Step 1 Label the bottom of the graph "Weekdays" and name the 5 weekdays that will be below the bars.

Step 2 Number the scale from 0 to 8 to show the number of birds. Label the scale "Number of Birds."

Step 3 Make bars for the days of the week shown in the table.

Step 4 Give the graph a title.

You will be using the table below to finish a bar graph.

Record Fish

Type of Fish	Weight of Largest One Caught
Bull trout	32 lb
Black skipjack	26 lb
Pollock	50 lb
Channel catfish	58 lb

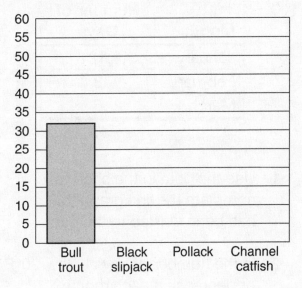

1. Complete the bar graph by drawing the rest of the bars. Insert labels and give your graph a title.

Making Line Graphs

The table shows the number of garbage cans emptied by a
truck for four days. Make a line graph to show how the number
changed from day to day.

Garbage Cans Emptied

Day	Number of Cans
1	20
2	40
3	30
4	15

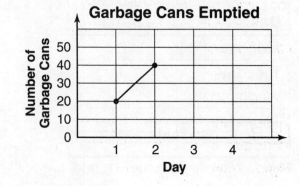

On the third day, 30 cans were emptied. Find the 3 at the
bottom of the graph and 30 along the side. Draw a point at the
place where 3 and 30 meet. Draw a line to connect that point
with the point for the second day.

Plot the point for the fourth day and draw a line to connect it to
the third day.

**Days Temperature
Below 20°F**

Month	Number of Days
January	12
February	8
March	6

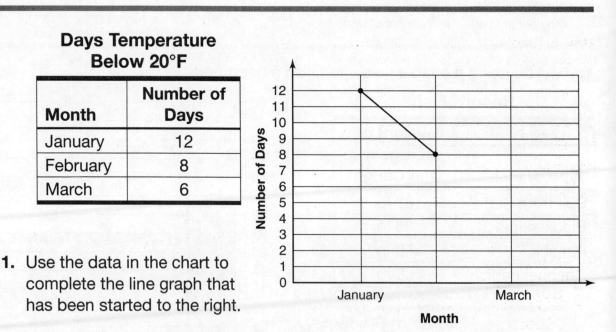

1. Use the data in the chart to
    complete the line graph that
    has been started to the right.

2. Is the number of days below 20°F increasing
    or decreasing each month?   _____

Name_____

PROBLEM-SOLVING STRATEGY
Make a Graph

Rainy Days Allison kept track of the number of rainy days for 5 months. How did the number of rainy days change over 5 months?

Month	Number of Rainy Days
April	10
May	7
June	3
July	7
August	5

Read and Understand

Step 1: What do you know?

I know the number of rainy days for 5 months.

Step 2: What are you trying to find?

I need to know how the number of rainy days changed over 5 months.

Plan and Solve

Step 3: What strategy will you use?

- I will enter all known data and look for a pattern.
- I will read the graph to answer the question.

Answer: There were 2 months when the number of rainy days was 7. June had the least number of rainy days. April had the most.

Strategy: Make a graph.

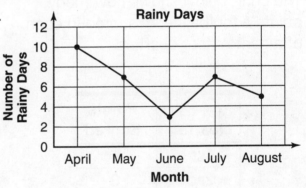

Look Back and Check

Is your work correct?

Yes, the graph shows the correct data.

---

1. Complete the pictograph. Use the data in the chart.

Sports Played by 3rd Graders

Sport	Number of Students
Softball	7
Hockey	14
Baseball	6
Tennis	8

Sports Played by 3rd Graders

Sport	Number of Students
Softball	
Hockey	
Baseball	
Tennis	

Each ⚊ = 2 students.

Problem-Solving Applications

Students' Favorite Dogs

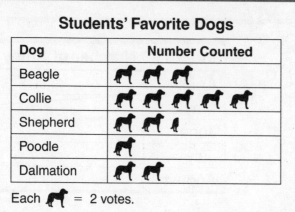

Dog	Number Counted
Beagle	🐕 🐕 🐕
Collie	🐕 🐕 🐕 🐕 🐕
Shepherd	🐕 🐕 🐾
Poodle	🐕
Dalmation	🐕 🐕

Each 🐕 = 2 votes.

Students were asked to tell their favorite kind of dog. This pictograph shows how many students chose each kind of dog as their favorite. Use the pictograph to answer each exercise.

How many students chose a beagle? 6 students

Which dog had 5 votes? Shepherd

The chart below shows how many points a football team scored in each of a game's four quarters.

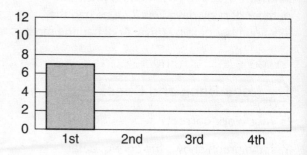

Quarter	Points Scored
1st	7
2nd	3
3rd	10
4th	6

1. Complete the bar graph.

2. How many points were scored in the 3rd quarter? _____

3. How many points were scored in the entire game? _____

Name_____

Multiplication as Repeated Addition

Each of the groups below has the same number of squares.
There are 5 groups of 4. There are a total of 20 squares.

Here is the addition sentence for this problem: $4 + 4 + 4 + 4 + 4 = 20$

Here is the multiplication sentence for this problem: $5 \times 4 = 20$

Complete the addition and multiplication sentences.

1.

4 groups of _____ $4 + 4 + 4 + 4 =$ _____ $4 \times$ _____ $= 16$

2.

_____ groups of 7   _____ + _____ + _____ + _____ = 28

$7 \times$ _____ = _____

Write each addition sentence as a multiplication sentence.

3. $1 + 1 + 1 + 1 + 1 = 5$ _____

4. $8 + 8 + 8 = 24$ _____

Write each multiplication sentence as an addition sentence.

5. $5 \times 5 = 25$ _____

6. $6 \times 2 = 12$ _____

7. Writing in Math Juan says, "When you put together unequal groups, you can only add." Is he correct? Explain.

_____

Arrays and Multiplication

An array shows objects in equal rows. This array shows 3 rows of 6 pennies.

The addition sentence for this array is
6 + 6 + 6 = 18.

The multiplication sentence for this array is
3 × 6 = 18.

Because of the Commutative (Order) Property of Multiplication, you can multiply the two numbers in any order:
3 × 6 = 18 and 6 × 3 = 18.

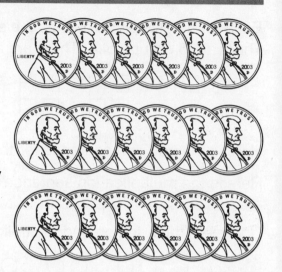

Write a multiplication sentence for each array.

1. O O O O O O O
   O O O O O O O   _____

2. ☐ ☐ ☐ ☐
   ☐ ☐ ☐ ☐
   ☐ ☐ ☐ ☐   _____
   ☐ ☐ ☐ ☐

Complete each multiplication sentence. You may use counters or draw a picture to help.

3. 3 × 4 = 12   _____ × 3 = 12   4. 5 × 2 = 10   2 × _____ = 10

5. **Number Sense** How can you use the commutative property to know that

O O O O O O
O O O O O O   is equal to
O O O O O O

O O O
O O O
O O O
O O O   ?
O O O
O O O

_____

_____

_____

Name_____

Writing Multiplication Stories

Name_____

Writing Multiplication Stories

R 5-3

When you write a multiplication story you should:

- Always end the story with a question.
- Draw a picture to show the main idea.

Example:

Write a multiplication story for 5 × 9.

Josephine has 5 friends over for a snack. She gives each friend 9 grapes. How many grapes did Josephine give altogether?

Josephine gave 45 grapes altogether.

Write a multiplication story for each exercise. Draw a picture to find each product.

1. 4 × 3

_____

_____

2. 5 × 2

_____

_____

3. 1 × 6

_____

_____

4. Number Sense Leshon mowed 7 lawns in his neighborhood. He made $5 for each lawn he mowed. Write a multiplication sentence to show how much money Leshon earned. _____

PROBLEM-SOLVING STRATEGY
Make a Table

Planting For every flower Tonya plants, she will need to water it with 2 gal of water. How many gallons of water will she need for 6 plants?

Read and Understand

Step 1: What do you know?
You know how much water is needed for each plant.

Step 2: What are you trying to find?
You are trying to find how many gallons of water are needed for 6 plants.

Plan and Solve

What strategy will you use?
Strategy: Make a table.

First, set up your table with labels.

Number of flowers						
Gallons of water						

Enter the information you know.

Number of flowers	1	2	3			
Gallons of water	2	4	6			

Look for a pattern. Continue the table.

Find the answer in the table.

Number of flowers	1	2	3	4	5	6
Gallons of water	2	4	6	8	10	12

Tonya will need 12 gal of water to plant 6 flowers.

Complete the table to solve the problem. Write the answer in a complete sentence.

1. Mrs. Dolan's nursery school class uses crayons during coloring time. Each student gets 6 crayons. If there are 6 students, how many crayons are needed?

Number of students	1	2	3	4	5	6
Number of crayons	6	12				

2 as a Factor

When you multiply by 2, you can think of an addition doubles fact. 2×3 is the same as 2 groups of 3 or $3 + 3$.

The table shows the multiplication facts for 2.

2s Facts	
$2 \times 0 = 0$	$2 \times 5 = 10$
$2 \times 1 = 2$	$2 \times 6 = 12$
$2 \times 2 = 4$	$2 \times 7 = 14$
$2 \times 3 = 6$	$2 \times 8 = 16$
$2 \times 4 = 8$	$2 \times 9 = 18$

Find 2×8.

What you **think**:   What you **write**:

2 groups of 8

$8 + 8 = 16$ $2 \times 8 = 16$

❘❘❘❘❘❘❘❘

❘❘❘❘❘❘❘❘

The products are also called multiples of 2.

Notice that each multiple of 2 ends in 0, 2, 4, 6, or 8. All multiples of 2 are even numbers, such as 34, 66, 78, and 102.

1. $1 \times 2 = $ _____

2. $3 \times 2 = $ _____

3. $2 \times \$4 = $ _____

4. $2 \times 5 = $ _____

5. $\$2 \times 1 = $ _____

6. $9 \times 2 = $ _____

7. $2 \times 2 = $ _____

8. $7 \times 2 = $ _____

9. $\$3 \times 2 = $ _____

10. $\begin{array}{r} \$2 \\ \times\ \ 9 \\ \hline \end{array}$

11. $\begin{array}{r} 6 \\ \times\ 2 \\ \hline \end{array}$

12. $\begin{array}{r} 2 \\ \times\ 8 \\ \hline \end{array}$

13. $\begin{array}{r} 2 \\ \times\ \$7 \\ \hline \end{array}$

14. Find the product of 2 and 3.   _____

15. Find 2 times 8.   _____

16. Multiply 9 and 2.   _____

17. **Writing in Math** Is 25 a multiple of 2? How do you know?

_____

_____

5 as a Factor

You can use patterns and skip counting to multiply by 5.

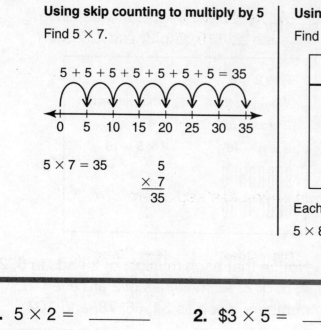

Using skip counting to multiply by 5

Find 5×7.

$$5 + 5 + 5 + 5 + 5 + 5 + 5 = 35$$

0 5 10 15 20 25 30 35

$5 \times 7 = 35$

$$\begin{array}{r} 5 \\ \times\ 7 \\ \hline 35 \end{array}$$

Using patterns to multiply by 5

Find 5×8.

5s Facts	
$5 \times 0 = 0$	$5 \times 5 = 25$
$5 \times 1 = 5$	$5 \times 6 = 30$
$5 \times 2 = 10$	$5 \times 7 = 35$
$5 \times 3 = 15$	$5 \times 8 = 40$
$5 \times 4 = 20$	$5 \times 9 = 45$

Each multiple of 5 ends in 0 or 5.

$5 \times 8 = 40$

---

1. $5 \times 2 =$ _____

2. $\$3 \times 5 =$ _____

3. $5 \times 8 =$ _____

4. $5 \times 6 =$ _____

5. $\$7 \times 5 =$ _____

6. $9 \times 5 =$ _____

7. $1 \times 5 =$ _____

8. $\$5 \times 5 =$ _____

9. $4 \times 5 =$ _____

10. $\begin{array}{r} 3 \\ \times\ 5 \\ \hline \end{array}$

11. $\begin{array}{r} \$5 \\ \times\ \ 4 \\ \hline \end{array}$

12. $\begin{array}{r} 9 \\ \times\ 5 \\ \hline \end{array}$

13. $\begin{array}{r} 5 \\ \times\ 7 \\ \hline \end{array}$

14. $\begin{array}{r} 2 \\ \times\ 8 \\ \hline \end{array}$

15. $\begin{array}{r} 5 \\ \times\ 5 \\ \hline \end{array}$

16. Yolanda has 8 nickels in her pocket. How much money does she have?

_____

17. **Algebra** What factors could you multiply to get a product of 25?

_____

10 as a Factor

The table shows the multiplication facts for 10.

10s Facts	
$10 \times 0 = 0$	$10 \times 5 = 50$
$10 \times 1 = 10$	$10 \times 6 = 60$
$10 \times 2 = 20$	$10 \times 7 = 70$
$10 \times 3 = 30$	$10 \times 8 = 80$
$10 \times 4 = 40$	$10 \times 9 = 90$

All multiples of 10 end with zero, such as 110; 2,350; and 467,000.

Find 10×5.

To find the answer, you can skip count or you can add a zero after the 5.

Tens	Ones		Tens	Ones
	5	$\times 10 =$	5	0

$5 \times 10 = 50$

---

1. $10 \times 2 =$ _____

2. $5 \times 10 =$ _____

3. $10 \times 8 =$ _____

4. $2 \times 8 =$ _____

5. $\$10 \times 6 =$ _____

6. $7 \times 5 =$ _____

7. $\$10 \times 4 =$ _____

8. $9 \times 2 =$ _____

9. $8 \times 9 =$ _____

10.
$$\begin{array}{r} 10 \\ \times\ 3 \\ \hline \end{array}$$

11.
$$\begin{array}{r} \$4 \\ \times\ 5 \\ \hline \end{array}$$

12.
$$\begin{array}{r} 2 \\ \times\ 2 \\ \hline \end{array}$$

13.
$$\begin{array}{r} \$10 \\ \times\ 6 \\ \hline \end{array}$$

14.
$$\begin{array}{r} \$8 \\ \times\ 5 \\ \hline \end{array}$$

15.
$$\begin{array}{r} 10 \\ \times\ 4 \\ \hline \end{array}$$

16. Number Sense Is 49 a multiple of 10? Explain.

_____

_____

PROBLEM-SOLVING SKILL
Multiple-Step Problems

Food Court Food court tickets cost $2 each. Susan bought a dinner and a dessert. How much did Susan spend?

Food Court Prices

Dinner	3 tickets
Dessert	2 tickets

Read and Understand

Find the hidden question.

How many tickets did Susan use?

> 3 + 2 = 5
> Susan used 5 tickets at the food court.

Plan and Solve

Solve the problem.

How much did Susan spend?

> 5 tickets × $2 = $10
> Susan spent $10 at the food court.

Write and answer the hidden question or questions. Then solve the problem. For 1–2, use the Balloon Prices list.

Balloon Prices		
Small	Medium	Large
$1.00	$2.00	$3.00

1. Virginia wants 3 large balloons. How much money will she need?

   _____

   _____

   _____

2. Reese buys 2 medium balloons and 2 small balloons. He pays with a $10 bill. How much change will Reese get?

   _____

   _____

   _____

   _____

   _____

Name _____

Multiplying with 0 and 1

Zero and 1 have special multiplication properties.

The Identity (One) Property of Multiplication	The Zero Property of Multiplication
When you multiply a number and 1, the product is that number. Examples: $4 \times 1 = 4$ $16 \times 1 = 16$ $1 \times 9 = 9$ $13 \times 1 = 13$ $251 \times 1 = 251$ $1 \times 48 = 48$	When you multiply a number and 0, the product is 0. Examples: $5 \times 0 = 0$ $123 \times 0 = 0$ $17 \times 0 = 0$ $0 \times 58 = 0$ $0 \times 51 = 0$ $74 \times 0 = 0$

1. $1 \times 2 = $ _____

2. $0 \times 3 = $ _____

3. $4 \times 1 = $ _____

4. $8 \times 0 = $ _____

5. $\$6 \times 1 = $ _____

6. $1 \times 7 = $ _____

7. $\$1$
    $\times \; 7$

8. 6
    $\times \; 0$

9. 8
    $\times \; 1$

10. $\$10$
     $\times \;\;\; 0$

11. $\$1$
     $\times \;\; 2$

12. 0
     $\times \; 9$

Complete each number sentence. Write <, >, or = for each $\bigcirc$.

13. $8 \times 2 \bigcirc 4 \times 4$ **14.** $19 \times 1 \bigcirc 37 \times 0$ **15.** $7 \times 2 \bigcirc 13 + 1$

Complete each number sentence. Write $\times$ or + for each $\bigcirc$.

16. $5 \bigcirc 0 = 5$ **17.** $5 \bigcirc 1 = 6$ **18.** $1 \bigcirc 5 = 5$

19. Writing in Math Write a multiplication sentence that shows the Zero Property of Multiplication. Explain why it shows this property.

_____

Name_____

9 as a Factor

Patterns can help you remember multiplication facts with 9 as a factor.

9s Facts
9 × 0 = 0
9 × 1 = 9
9 × 2 = 18
9 × 3 = 27
9 × 4 = 36
9 × 5 = 45
9 × 6 = 54
9 × 7 = 63
9 × 8 = 72
9 × 9 = 81

Here is one pattern: The tens digit is always 1 less than the factor multiplied by 9.

For example:

9 × 6 = 54. The factor 6 is multiplied by 9. One less than 6 is 5. The tens digit is 5.

Here is another pattern: The sum of the digits of the product always add to 9.

For example:

9 × 5 = 45   9 × 3 = 27
4 + 5 = 9   2 + 7 = 9

Find 9 × 7.

Use the patterns to help you find the answer.

7 − 1 = 6. The tens digit will be 6.
9 − 6 = 3. The ones digit will be 3.
9 × 7 = 63

1. 9 × 3 = _____   2. 2 × 9 = _____   3. $9 × 2 = _____

4. 4 × 2 = _____   5. 9 × 10 = _____   6. 6 × 5 = _____

7. 9 × 8 = _____   8. $2 × 2 = _____   9. 6 × $9 = _____

10. $9   11.   10   12.   9
    × 9   × 6   × 0

13. Multiply 9 and 7.   _____

14. **Writing in Math** Look at the table of 9s facts. Can you think of another number pattern in the multiples of 9? Explain.

_____

_____

68 Use with Lesson 5-10.

Practicing Multiplication Facts

Here is how to make a set of flashcards.

- Write the first part of a multiplication fact on the front of the card.
- Write the product on the back.

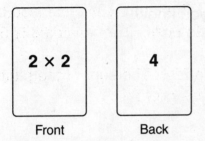

Front   Back

Invite a partner to make a set of 10 flashcards while you also make 10 flashcards. Use them to play a game together. Hold a flashcard so that the multiplication fact (the front) faces your partner and the product (the back) faces you. Have your partner say the product without looking at the back of the flashcard. Take turns holding the flashcards for each other.

1. $4 \times 9 = $ _____   **2.** $2 \times 6 = $ _____   **3.** $5 \times 4 = $ _____

4. $10 \times 2 = $ _____   **5.** $6 \times 1 = $ _____   **6.** $2 \times 7 = $ _____

7. $9 \times 8 = $ _____   **8.** $7 \times 1 = $ _____   **9.** $6 \times 1 = $ _____

10. $2 \times 7 = $ _____   **11.** $9 \times 8 = $ _____   **12.** $7 \times 1 = $ _____

13.   9
    $\times\ 7$

14.   5
    $\times\ 5$

15.   9
    $\times\ 3$

16.   5
    $\times\ 2$

17. Number Sense Shawna thinks that $8 \times 2 = 17$. What number pattern shows that she is not correct?

_____

Algebra Write the missing number.

18. $10 \times$ _____ $= 50$ **19.** $9 \times$ _____ $= 36$ **20.** _____ $\times 5 = 45$

Name_____

Dozens of Eggs!

At United States chicken farms, female chickens lay about 5 eggs per week. How many eggs would the chicken lay after 6 weeks?

You can make a table to solve this problem.

First, draw your table and enter the information you know.

Week	1	2	3	4	5	6
Eggs laid	5					

Then look for a pattern and continue the table.

Week	1	2	3	4	5	6
Eggs laid	5	10	15	20	25	30

After 6 weeks, the chicken will have laid about 30 eggs.

1. Tim collects eggs each morning on his family farm. If he collects 7 eggs each morning, how many eggs will he have after 7 days? Complete the table to solve this problem.

Day	1	2	3	4	5	6	7
Eggs collected	7						

2. Suppose there are 2 eggs in a carton. How many eggs will you have if you buy 3 cartons? 7 cartons? 9 cartons?

_____

3. Suppose there are 5 eggs in a carton. How many eggs will you have if you buy 4 cartons? 8 cartons? 10 cartons?

_____

4. Suppose there are 9 eggs in a carton. How many eggs will you have if you buy 5 cartons? 7 cartons? 9 cartons?

_____

3 as a Factor

You can use an array to show multiplication. The number of rows is the first factor, and the number of columns is the second factor.

What You Show   **What You Think**

(1)

(3) ● ● ● $3 \times 1 = 3$

(2)

(2) ●● ●● $2 \times 2 = 4$
    ●● ●●

Complete the arrays.

$3 \times 5 =$ _____

● ● ● ● ●
● ● ● ● ● $2 \times$ _____ $=$ _____

● ● ● ● ● $1 \times$ _____ $=$ _____

                   $3 \times$ _____ $= 15$

---

1. $3 \times 2 =$ _____   **2.** $3 \times 4 =$ _____   **3.** $3 \times 5 =$ _____

4. $\begin{array}{r} 3 \\ \times\ 8 \\ \hline \end{array}$ **5.** $\begin{array}{r} 3 \\ \times\ 9 \\ \hline \end{array}$ **6.** $\begin{array}{r} 7 \\ \times\ 3 \\ \hline \end{array}$

7. Number Sense Each of 3 dogs has 6 puppies.
How many puppies are there altogether?   _____

Name_____

4 as a Factor

R 6-2

If you know a 2s multiplication fact, you can find a 4s multiplication fact.

When you double an array of 2 × 1, you get an array of 4 × 1.

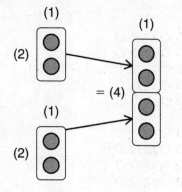

This shows that if you double a 2s fact, or add the
2s fact to itself, you can find the 4s fact.

$(2 \times 1) + (2 \times 1) = (4 \times 1)$
$2 + 2 = 4$

---

1. 4 × 1 = _____

2. 4 × 2 = _____

3. 4 × 7 = _____

4. 4 × 3 = _____

5.　　4
　　× 9

6.　　4
　　× 6

7.　　5
　　× 4

8.　　4
　　× $8

9. Number Sense How can you use 2 × 10 to find 4 × 10?

_____

_____

_____

_____

6 and 7 as Factors

You can use multiplication facts that you already know to find multiplication facts you are unsure of.
You know the multiplication facts for 1s, 2s, and 5s.

Find 9×6.

Break apart an array for 9×6 into two separate arrays. Make one array for 5×6 in order to use your knowledge of 5s facts. Make the second array 4×6.

$5 \times 6 = 30$

$4 \times 6 = 24$

$30 + 24 = 54$, so $9 \times 6 = 54$

Find 7×8.

You can do the same thing to multiply by 7.
Break the array for 7×8 into two separate arrays:
one for 5×8 and one for 2×8.

$5 \times 8 = 40$

$2 \times 8 = 16$

$40 + 16 = 56$, so $7 \times 8 = 56$

1. $2 \times 7 =$ _____

2. $5 \times 7 =$ _____

3. $7 \times 9 =$ _____

4. $6 \times 4 =$ _____

5. $6 \times 6 =$ _____

6. $6 \times \$10 =$ _____

7. $\begin{array}{r} 4 \\ \times\ 7 \\ \hline \end{array}$

8. $\begin{array}{r} 8 \\ \times\ 6 \\ \hline \end{array}$

9. $\begin{array}{r} \$7 \\ \times\ 3 \\ \hline \end{array}$

10. $\begin{array}{r} 5 \\ \times\ 9 \\ \hline \end{array}$

11. Number Sense Harold says "To find 6×8, I can use the facts for 5×4 and 1×4." Do you agree? Explain.

_____

_____

8 as a Factor

You can use doubling to help multiply with 8.

Find 8 × 6.

You can double a 4s fact to multiply with 8.

First, find 4 × 6 = 24.

Then double the product.

$$\left.\begin{array}{c} \circ\circ\circ\circ\circ\circ \\ \circ\circ\circ\circ\circ\circ \\ \circ\circ\circ\circ\circ\circ \\ \circ\circ\circ\circ\circ\circ \end{array}\right\} 4 \times 6 = 24$$

24 + 24 = 48

$$\left.\begin{array}{c} \circ\circ\circ\circ\circ\circ \\ \circ\circ\circ\circ\circ\circ \\ \circ\circ\circ\circ\circ\circ \\ \circ\circ\circ\circ\circ\circ \end{array}\right\} 4 \times 6 = 24$$

So, 8 × 6 = 48.

Find 8 × 8.

$$\begin{array}{r} 4 \times 8 = 32 \\ \underline{4 \times 8 = 32} \\ 8 \times 8 = 64 \end{array}$$

---

1. 2 × 8 = _____

2. 4 × 8 = _____

3. 8 × 5 = _____

4. 5 × 6 = _____

5. 0
    × 8
———

6. 8
    × 3
———

7. 9
    × 8
———

8. 8
   × 10
———

9. Number Sense Name a multiplication fact that can help you with 8 × 4, and tell how.

_____

_____

Practicing Multiplication Facts

You can use more than one strategy to find the same multiplication fact.

Find 6×4.

You can switch the order of the factors in a multiplication problem and still have the same result. 6×4 is the same as 4×6. If you know the fact that $4 \times 6 = 24$, then you also know the fact that $6 \times 4 = 24$. This is called the Commutative Property of Addition.

Some facts can be added to find facts that you do not know. You can combine 5×4 and 1×4 to find 6×4. $5 \times 4 = 20$ and $1 \times 4 = 4$. $20 + 4 = 24$, so $6 \times 4 = 24$.

Some facts can be doubled to find facts that you do not know.
2s facts can be doubled to find 4s facts.
4s facts can be doubled to find 8s facts.

6×4 is the same as 4×6. Double the 2s fact for 6. $6 \times 2 = 12$.
12 doubled is 24. $6 \times 4 = 24$.

1. $2 \times 9 =$ _____

2. $5 \times 7 =$ _____

3. $5 \times 8 =$ _____

4. $7 \times 8 =$ _____

5.   6
  $\times\ 5$

6.   4
  $\times\ 9$

7.   5
  $\times\ 9$

8.   8
  $\times\ 6$

9. **Number Sense** Darien does not know the fact for 6×5.
Tell two ways that will help him find the product without adding together five 6s.

_____

_____

_____

_____

Look for a Pattern

Dots Pattern Here is a pattern with dots. What will the 5th and 6th pictures look like?

1st   2nd   3rd   4th   5th   6th

Read and Understand

Step 1: What do you know?

The number of dots in the first four pictures.

Step 2: What are you trying to find?

The number of dots for the 5th and 6th pictures.

Plan and Solve

Step 3: What strategy will you use?

There are 3 more dots in the 2nd picture than in the 1st picture.

Strategy: Look for a pattern.

There are 3 more dots in the 3rd picture than in the 2nd picture.

The number of dots increases by 3 each time.

Answer: There will be 13 dots in the 5th picture and 16 dots in the 6th picture.

Look Back and Check

Step 4: Is your work correct?

Yes, the "increases by 3" pattern works for all of the pictures.

Complete the pattern. Then tell what the pattern is.

1. ○ □ △ △ ○ __ __

_____

_____

2. What are the missing numbers in the pattern below?

3, 8, 13, _____, _____, 28, _____

_____

Name_____

Using Multiplication to Compare

The word *times* in a word problem means multiplication. If you
have 3 times as many pencils as Joe does, it means that however
many pencils Joe has, you have his pencils multiplied by 3.

Pencil	Pencil					⟶ Number of pencils

Pencil	Pencil	Pencil	Pencil	Pencil	Pencil	⟶ 3 times as many pencils

The words *twice as many* or *2 times as many* mean to multiply by 2.

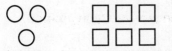

There are twice as many squares as there are circles.

---

1. Sara has twice as many ribbons as Harriet.
   Harriet has 6 ribbons. How many ribbons
   does Sarah have?   _____

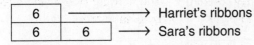

6		⟶ Harriet's ribbons
6	6	⟶ Sara's ribbons

2. Luke is 6 years old. Danny is 3 times
   his age. How old is Danny?   _____

3. Paula has 3 rings. Kenya has 4 times as many
   rings. How many rings does Kenya have?   _____

4. **Number Sense** If Leroy has 9 sports cards,
   and Steve has 3 times as many, how many
   sports cards does Steve have?   _____

5. Jill invited 6 friends to her party. Mara invited
   twice as many to her sleepover. How many
   friends were invited to Mara's sleepover?   _____

Patterns on a Table

Use the fact table to find 9×5. Find the 9 across the top and count down 6 spaces. Then find the 5 along the side and count across 10 spaces. The box where the column and the row meet is the product. For 9×5, follow the 9s column down and the 5s row across. The box where they meet is 45, so $9 \times 5 = 45$.

×	0	1	2	3	4	5	6	7	8	9	10	11	12
0	0	0	0	0	0	0	0	0	0	0	0	0	0
1	0	1	2	3	4	5	6	7	8	9	10	11	12
2	0	2	4	6	8	10	12	14	16	18	20	22	24
3	0	3	6	9	12	15	18	21	24	27	30	33	36
4	0	4	8	12	16	20	24	28	32	36	40	44	48
5	0	5	10	15	20	25	30	35	40	45	50	55	60
6	0	6	12	18	24	30	36	42	48	54	60	66	72
7	0	7	14	21	28	35	42	49	56	63	70	77	84
8	0	8	16	24	32	40	48	56	64	72	80	88	96
9	0	9	18	27	36	45	54	63	72	81	90	99	108
10	0	10	20	30	40	50	60	70	80	90	100	110	120
11	0	11	22	33	44	55	66	77	88	99	110	121	132
12	0	12	24	36	48	60	72	84	96	108	120	132	144

1. $4 \times 7 = $ _____

2. $5 \times 3 = $ _____

3. $0 \times 4 = $ _____

4. $3 \times 6 = $ _____

5. $\begin{array}{r} 7 \\ \times\ 2 \\ \hline \end{array}$

6. $\begin{array}{r} 1 \\ \times\ 5 \\ \hline \end{array}$

7. $\begin{array}{r} 9 \\ \times\ 3 \\ \hline \end{array}$

8. $\begin{array}{r} 6 \\ \times\ 7 \\ \hline \end{array}$

9. **Writing in Math** Skye has 6 bags of balloons. Each bag contains 4 balloons. How many balloons does Skye have altogether? Explain how you can use the multiplication table to help find the answer.

_____

_____

Multiplying with Three Factors

When more than two factors are being multiplied, you can multiply them in any order and the product will be the same. This is called the Associative (grouping) Property of Multiplication.

Here are three different ways to multiply $6 \times 5 \times 4$.

Multiply the 6 and 5 first.	Multiply the 5 and 4 first.	Multiply the 6 and 4 first.
$(6 \times 5) \times 4$	$6 \times (5 \times 4)$	$(6 \times 4) \times 5$
$30 \times 4 = 120$	$6 \times 20 = 120$	$24 \times 5 = 120$

In each example, the product is the same. This means that you can find the easiest way to multiply more than two numbers.

---

1. $3 \times 2 \times 1 =$ _____

2. $2 \times 3 \times 5 =$ _____

3. $3 \times 3 \times 2 =$ _____

4. $7 \times 2 \times 1 =$ _____

5. $4 \times 7 \times 2 =$ _____

6. $5 \times 1 \times 2 =$ _____

7. $5 \times 2 \times 4 =$ _____

8. $4 \times 0 \times 3 =$ _____

9. $1 \times 0 \times 4 =$ _____

10. $3 \times 4 \times 5 =$ _____

11. $1 \times 4 \times 6 =$ _____

12. $2 \times 2 \times 6 =$ _____

13. $4 \times 1 \times 7 =$ _____

14. $8 \times 2 \times 1 =$ _____

15. **Number Sense** How do you know that $4 \times 2 \times 2$ is the same as 4×4? Explain.

_____

_____

_____

Find a Rule

David is cooking pancakes. He makes 3 pancakes for each person in his family. Today he needs to make pancakes for 9 people. He isn't sure how many he needs to make. If David used a table, he would see a rule for a pattern between the number of pancakes and the number of people eating those pancakes.

Number of people	1	2	3
Number of pancakes	3	6	

The rule for the pattern is multiply by 3. To make pancakes for 9 people, he takes the number of people, 9, and follows the rule, multiply by 3, to find that he needs to make 27 pancakes.

Write a rule for each table. Complete the table.

1.

Number of tents	1	2	3	4	5
Number of hikers	4	8	12		

_____

2.

In	3	4	1	2	7
Out	15	20	5		

_____

3.

In	2	4	6	8	10
Out	14	28			

_____

4. Number Sense Chris can sand 7 planks in 1 hour. How many planks can he sand in 3 hours?

_____

Name_____

Choose an Operation

New Restaurant A new restaurant opened and hired 2 new people a day for the first 6 days. How many new people were hired?

Read and Understand

Show the main idea.

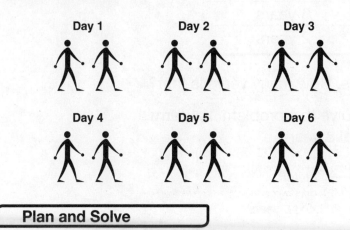

Day 1   Day 2   Day 3

Day 4   Day 5   Day 6

Plan and Solve

Choose an operation.

Multiply to find the total when you put together equal groups.

$6 \times 2 = 12$

So, 12 new people were hired.

Draw a picture to show the main idea. Choose an operation, and solve the problem.

1. Every student who earned more than $100 for his or her school in a fund drive was given 4 movie passes. There were 8 students at the school who earned over $100. How many movie passes were given out at the school?

Name_____

Terms

The word *term* means how long a person will perform an elected duty. The chart below shows how long a term is for the president, senators, and representatives of the United States government.

Elected Position	Term
President	4 years
Senator	6 years
U.S. representative	2 years

A president can only serve 2 terms. How many years is that?

You would use multiplication to solve this problem. If 1 term equals 4 years, then 2 terms equal 8 years.

4 years		$\longrightarrow$ 1 term
4 years	4 years	$\longrightarrow$ $2 \times 4 = 8$ years

---

1. For how many years would a representative serve if he or she served 3 terms?   _____

2. If a representative served 5 terms, how many years would it be?   _____

3. In 1991, the state of Colorado passed a law stating that a U.S. representative from that state could serve a maximum of 6 terms. How many years equal 6 terms?   _____

4. If a senator serves 7 terms, how many years would it be?   _____

5. **Number Sense** Which is longer, 2 terms as senator or 7 terms as a representative? How do you know?

_____

_____

Name_____

Division as Sharing

R 7-1

You can use counters to show division problems:

There are 6 shirts and 3 boxes. How many shirts fit in each box?

First, use 6 counters for the 6 shirts.	Since the problem is 6 divided by 3, divide the counters into 3 groups.	There are 2 counters in each group. Since 6 ÷ 3 = 2, two shirts can fit in each box.

Use counters or draw a picture to solve.

1. 12 markers   3 boxes

How many markers in each box?

_____

2. 10 pencils   2 pencil cases

How many pencils in each pencil case?

_____

3. 9 tadpoles   3 tanks

How many tadpoles in each tank?

_____

4. 16 marbles   4 sacks

How many marbles in each sack?

_____

5. Number Sense Could you divide 14 shirts into two equal groups? Why or why not?

_____

_____

Division as Repeated Subtraction

You can also think of division as repeated subtraction. Here is an example:

Joe has 15 sweaters. He is packing them into boxes. Each box holds 3 sweaters. How many boxes does Joe need?

Start with 15 sweaters. Subtract 3 at a time until there are no sweaters left. Then count the subtractions.

$15 - 3 = 12$

$12 - 3 = 9$

$9 - 3 = 6$

$6 - 3 = 3$

$3 - 3 = 0$

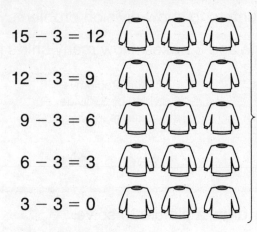

I can subtract three 5 times. Then there are zero sweaters left over.

You can also use division.
$15 \div 3 = 5$
Fifteen divided by 3 equals 5.
Joe needs 5 boxes.

Use counters or draw a picture to solve.

1. 10 markers   5 markers in each box

   How many boxes? _____

2. 20 books   5 books on each shelf

   How many shelves? _____

3. 8 hamsters   2 hamsters in each cage

   How many cages? _____

4. **Writing in Math** Show how you can use repeated subtraction to find how many groups of 3 are in 18. Then write the division sentence for the problem.

   _____

   _____

   _____

Writing Division Stories

How to write a division story:

First, look at the number sentence given. Think of a situation in which the larger number is divided by the smaller number. For example, with the number sentence $20 \div 2 = n$, you might think of 20 dollars divided between 2 friends. Here is a division story for $20 \div 2 = n$:

> Dan's father gave him $20 for cutting the grass and doing other chores around the house. Since Dan's friend Steve helped him, Dan decided to divide the money by 2. How much did each boy receive?

Write a division story for each. Then use counters or draw a picture to solve.

1. $15 \div 3 = n$

_____

_____

_____

2. $12 \div 2 = n$

_____

_____

_____

3. Number Sense Sheila wrote a story problem. In her story, she asked how many equal groups 16 flowers could be put in. What does she need to tell about the groups?

_____

_____

_____

Name_____

Try, Check, and Revise

New Pencils Stephanie needs 15 pencils for school. Pencils
come in packs of 4, 5, or 6. If she wants to buy 3 equal-sized
packs of pencils, what size pack of pencils should she buy?

Read and Understand

Step 1: What do you know? She needs 15 pencils. Pencils come in packs of 4, 5, or 6.

Step 2: What are you trying to find? Find what size pack she needs to buy to have 3 equal-sized
packs.

Plan and Solve

Step 3: What strategy will you use? Try, check, and revise

Try: packs of 4

Check: $4 + 4 + 4 = 12$ Too low

Revise: packs of 5

Check: $5 + 5 + 5 = 15$ That's it!

Look Back and Check

Step 4: Is your answer reasonable? Yes, 3 packs of 5 pencils equal 15 pencils.

Solve. Write each answer in a sentence.

1. There are 12 fish in Zack's aquarium. He has 2 kinds of
   fish: guppies and tetras. He has 4 more guppies than
   tetras. How many of each kind of fish does he have?

   _____

2. The sum of two numbers is 33. Both numbers are less than
   20. The numbers are 3 apart. What are the numbers?

   _____

Relating Multiplication and Division

You can use what you know about multiplication to understand division. Fact families show how multiplication and division are related.

Here is the fact family for 3, 8, and 24:

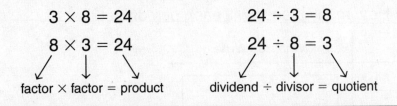

$3 \times 8 = 24$ $24 \div 3 = 8$

$8 \times 3 = 24$ $24 \div 8 = 3$

factor × factor = product   dividend ÷ divisor = quotient

Complete. Use counters or draw a picture to solve.

1. $3 \times$ _____ $= 6$

   $6 \div 3 =$ _____

2. $7 \times$ _____ $= 14$

   $14 \div 7 =$ _____

3. $5 \times$ _____ $= 20$

   $20 \div 5 =$ _____

4. $4 \times$ _____ $= 24$

   $24 \div 4 =$ _____

5. Number Sense What other number is a part of this fact family? 3, 4, _____

6. There are 28 days in 4 weeks. What fact family would you use to find the number of days in 1 week?

_____

7. There are 12 in. in 1 ft. What fact family would you use to find the number of inches in 2 ft?

_____

Dividing with 2 and 5

Thinking about multiplication can help you divide with 2 and 5.

For example:

Darren and Molly have 16 pieces of construction paper for their project. Each person will get the same number of pieces of construction paper. How many pieces will each person get?

What You **Think**	What You **Write**
Find $16 \div 2$. 2 times what number equals 16? $2 \times 8 = 16$	$16 \div 2 = 8$ So, each person will get 8 pieces of construction paper.

Solve.

1. $30 \div 5 =$ _____

2. $12 \div 2 =$ _____

3. $35 \div 5 =$ _____

4. $16 \div 2 =$ _____

5. Number Sense Write a fact family that would help you solve $15 \div 5 = n$.

_____

6. How many nickels equal one quarter? _____
What multiplication fact can you use to help solve this problem?

_____

7. How many dimes equal one half-dollar? _____
What multiplication fact can you use to help solve this problem?

_____

Coins	
Penny	1 cent
Nickel	5 cents
Dime	10 cents
Quarter	25 cents
Half-dollar	50 cents

8. How many quarters equal one half-dollar? _____

Dividing with 3 and 4

You can use multiplication facts for 3 and 4 to help you divide by 3 or 4.

Problem	Peter has 32 planks. If he places them in four equal piles, how many planks will be in each pile?	May and her two friends have 21 treats. If each person gets an equal amount, how many treats does each girl get?
What You **Think**	Four times what number equals 32? $4 \times 8 = 32$	Three times what number equals 21? $3 \times 7 = 21$
What You **Write**	$32 \div 4 = 8$ There will be 8 planks in each pile.	$21 \div 3 = 7$ Each girl gets 7 treats.

You can write a division problem in two ways:

$$32 \div 4 = 8 \qquad \textbf{or} \qquad 4)\overline{32}$$

dividend divisor quotient   divisor dividend

8 ← quotient

---

1. $30 \div 3 =$ _____

2. $20 \div 4 =$ _____

3. $15 \div 3 =$ _____

4. $4)\overline{40}$

5. $3)\overline{18}$

6. $4)\overline{28}$

7. Number Sense What multiplication fact could help you find $27 \div 3$?

_____

8. Ms. Johnson's class has 24 students. Could Ms. Johnson place her class into 3 equal-sized groups? _____

9. How many students would be in each of the 3 groups? _____

Name_____

Dividing with 6 and 7

When you divide, you separate things into equal groups.

For example:

Find $35 \div 7$.

There are 35 circles.

Divide them into
7 equal groups.

There are 5 circles
in each group.
So $35 \div 7 = 5$

```
OOOOOOOOO
OOOOOOOOO
OOOOOOOOO
OOOOOOOO
```

---

1. $30 \div 6 =$ _____

2. $28 \div 7 =$ _____

3. $42 \div 6 =$ _____

4. $7\overline{)49}$

5. $6\overline{)24}$

6. $6\overline{)12}$

7. Number Sense Name a number that can be equally
divided into groups of 6 and groups of 7.   _____

There are several different ways a football team
can score points. Two of the ways are shown
in the table.

Play	Points
Touchdown	6
Touchdown with extra point	7

8. If a football team has scored 3 times and
has a total of 18 points, how did they score
each time?

_____

9. If a football team has scored 3 times and has a total of
19 points, how did they score each time?

_____

_____

Name_____

Dividing with 8 and 9

Remembering multiplication facts can help you divide by 8 and 9.

What multiplication fact can help you find 24 ÷ 8?

8 x 1 = 8	8 x 6 = 48
8 x 2 = 16	8 x 7 = 56
(8 x 3 = 24)	8 x 8 = 64
8 x 4 = 32	8 x 9 = 72
8 x 5 = 40	8 x 10 = 80

If 8 × 3 = 24, then 24 ÷ 8 = 3.

What multiplication fact can help you find 27 ÷ 9?

9 x 1 = 9	9 x 6 = 54
9 x 2 = 18	9 x 7 = 63
(9 x 3 = 27)	9 x 8 = 72
9 x 4 = 36	9 x 9 = 81
9 x 5 = 45	9 x 10 = 90

If 9 × 3 = 27, then 27 ÷ 9 = 3.

---

1. 32 ÷ 8 = _____   **2.** 54 ÷ 9 = _____   **3.** 48 ÷ 8 = _____

4. 9)72   **5.** 9)63   **6.** 8)56

7. Number Sense What multiplication fact could
you use to find a number that can be divided
equally by 8 and by 9?   _____

8. From 1912 until the beginning of 1959, the United
States had 48 states. The flag at that time had
48 stars, one for each state. The 48 stars on the
flag were arranged in 6 equal rows. How many
stars were in each row?   _____

Use with Lesson 7-9. **91**

Name_____

Dividing with 0 and 1

There are special rules to follow when dividing by 1 or 0.

Rule	Example	What You **Think**	What You **Write**
When any number is divided by 1, the quotient is that number.	$7 \div 1 = ?$	1 times what number = 7? $1 \times 7 = 7$ So, $7 \div 1 = 7$	$7 \div 1 = 7$ or $1\overline{)7}$ with quotient 7
When any number (except 0) is divided by itself, the quotient is 1.	$8 \div 8 = ?$	8 times what number = 8? $8 \times 1 = 8$ So, $8 \div 8 = 1$	$8 \div 8 = 1$ or $8\overline{)8}$ with quotient 1
When zero is divided by a number (except 0), the quotient is 0.	$0 \div 5 = ?$	5 times what number = 0? $5 \times 0 = 0$ So, $0 \div 5 = 0$	$0 \div 5 = 0$ or $5\overline{)0}$ with quotient 0
You cannot divide a number by 0.	$9 \div 0 = ?$	0 times what number = 9? There is no number that works, so $9 \div 0$ cannot be done.	$9 \div 0$ cannot be done

1. $25 \div 1 = $ _____

2. $9 \div 9 = $ _____

3. $0 \div 8 = $ _____

4. $1\overline{)7}$

5. $12\overline{)12}$

6. $0\overline{)17}$

Compare. Use $<$, $>$, or $=$.

7. $15 \div 1 \bigcirc 15 \div 15$

8. $0 \div 12 \bigcirc 12 \div 12$

9. $8 \div 1 \bigcirc 8 \div 1$

10. $1 \div 1 \bigcirc 0 \div 1$

92 Use with Lesson 7-10.

Remainders

Keith has 21 sports cards. Each plastic sleeve holds 6 cards. How many sleeves will be filled? Will there be any cards left over?

Find 21 ÷ 6.

What You **Do**	What You **Write**
Draw a picture to show the main idea of the problem.	21 ÷ 6 = 3 R3
	3 R3 is read "three remainder three."
There are 3 groups of 6 with 3 left over. The remainder is 3.	Keith filled 3 sleeves. He has 3 cards left over.

Use counters or draw a picture to find each quotient and remainder.

1. 16 ÷ 5 = _____   **2.** 14 ÷ 3 = _____   **3.** 19 ÷ 8 = _____

4. 17 ÷ 4 = _____   **5.** 8 ÷ 3 = _____   **6.** 11 ÷ 7 = _____

7. Number Sense Jamal divided 16 by 5. His answer was 2 R6. Is his answer correct? If not, what is the correct answer?

_____

There are 50 states in the United States. Mr. Hernandez's students are going to study each state.

8. Mr. Hernandez has assigned a group of 8 students to write paragraphs about the states. If the group of 8 students needs to write a paragraph about each of the 50 states, can the work be divided evenly among the students in the group?   _____

If not, how many states are left over?   _____

Division Patterns with 10, 11, and 12 R 7-12

A number is divisible by another number when it can be divided by that number and the remainder is 0. For example, $80 \div 10 = 8$. You can also say that 80 is a **multiple** of 10. The chart below shows the multiples of 10, 11, and 12.

×	0	1	2	3	4	5	6	7	8	9	10	11	12
0	0	0	0	0	0	0	0	0	0	0	0	0	0
1	0	1	2	3	4	5	6	7	8	9	10	11	12
2	0	2	4	6	8	10	12	14	16	18	20	22	24
3	0	3	6	9	12	15	18	21	24	27	30	33	36
4	0	4	8	12	16	20	24	28	32	36	40	44	48
5	0	5	10	15	20	25	30	35	40	45	50	55	60
6	0	6	12	18	24	30	36	42	48	54	60	66	72
7	0	7	14	21	28	35	42	49	56	63	70	77	84
8	0	8	16	24	32	40	48	56	64	72	80	88	96
9	0	9	18	27	36	45	54	63	72	81	90	99	108
10	0	10	20	30	40	50	60	70	80	90	100	110	120
11	0	11	22	33	44	55	66	77	88	99	110	121	132
12	0	12	24	36	48	60	72	84	96	108	120	132	144

- The numbers 0, 10, 20, ..., 120 are all multiples of 10. Each of these numbers is divisible by 10. For example, $30 \div 10 = 3$.

- The numbers 0, 11, 22, ..., 132 are all multiples of 11. Each of these numbers is divisible by 11. For example, $99 \div 11 = 9$.

- The numbers 0, 12, 24, ..., 144 are all multiples of 12. Each of these numbers is divisible by 12. For example, $108 \div 12 = 9$.

Find each quotient. You may use a multiplication table, counters, or draw a picture to help.

1. $48 \div 12 = $ _____

2. $50 \div 10 = $ _____

3. $44 \div 11 = $ _____

4. $11\overline{)66}$

5. $10\overline{)20}$

6. $12\overline{)48}$

7. Writing in Math Explain how you can use skip counting to find $70 \div 10$.

_____

_____

Name_____

Translating Words to Expressions

Family Kay has 5 fewer aunts than cousins. She has 15 cousins. Write a numerical expression that shows how many aunts and cousins Kay has total.

The words in the problem give you clues about the operation.

Word or Phrase	Use
Total	+
Difference of	−
Times	×
Half; placed into equal groups	÷

Since Kay has 15 cousins, and 5 fewer aunts than cousins, she must have 10 aunts. The numerical expression that shows the total number of aunts and cousins she has is 10 + 15.

Write the numerical expression for each word phrase.

1. 14 baseball cards placed into 2 equal groups   _____

2. 12 more than 85   _____

3. 6 times as long as 7   _____

4. 3 times as old as 5   _____

5. the total of 4 cats and 15 dogs   _____

6. $14 less than $44   _____

7. **Writing in Math** Write a word phrase for this numerical expression: 8 × 5.

_____

_____

Name_____

The Student Musicians

The fifth- and sixth-grade string music students at Highland Elementary gave a concert. Several different groups of student musicians played songs. One of the groups had 4 members. Their instruments had a total of 20 strings. What instruments could these group members be playing?

String Instruments

Instrument	Number of Strings
Violin	4
Viola	4
Cello	4
Bass	4
Guitar	6

Try: First, try 1 guitar and 3 violins.

Check: 3 violins × 4 strings each = 12 strings, plus 6 guitar strings equals 18 strings. This answer is too low by 2 strings.

Revise: I'll try 2 violins and 2 guitars. This should give me 20 strings. 4 × 2 = 8, 6 × 2 = 12, 12 + 8 = 20.

This answer works. I have 4 string players and 20 strings.

---

1. There are a total of 32 string players in the fifth and sixth grades. There are 6 more fifth graders than sixth graders. How many string players are in each grade?

    _____

2. The 32 string players often play in groups of 4 players. How many groups of 4 players could they form?

    _____

3. If the string players are divided into groups of 6 players, are

    there any students left over? _____ If so, how many? _____

4. The string players played a concert that included 5 songs. The songs were all the same length. The concert lasted 30 min. How long was each song?

    _____

Name_____

Solid Figures

R 8-1

Three-dimensional objects are called solid figures. Solid figures are found in the world in many shapes and sizes.

The battery is an example of a cylinder. A **solid figure** is named according to its features.

 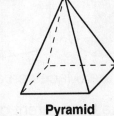

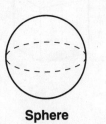
Sphere

Cone

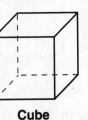
Cube

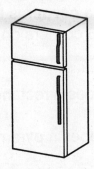
Rectangular Prism

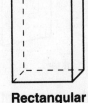
Pyramid

Name the solid figure or figures each object looks like.

1.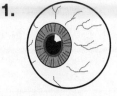

_____

2.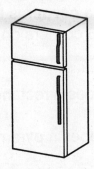

_____

3.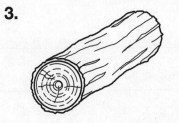

_____

4.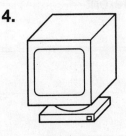

_____

Relating Solids and Shapes

In a drawing of a solid figure, it is not always easy to find the number of faces, edges, or corners. Sometimes it helps to imagine that the solid figure is transparent.

By using a transparent cube, you can count each face. Remember that each flat surface is called a **face.**

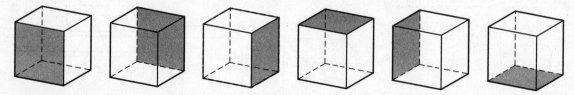

There are 6 faces on a cube.

Use the transparent cube to count the number of edges. Remember that an **edge** is a line segment where two faces meet. There are 12 edges on a cube.

Can you use the transparent cube to find the number of corners on a cube? Remember a **corner** is the point where 2 or more edges meet. There are 8 corners on a cube.

1. How many faces does a rectangular prism have? _____

2. How many edges does a pyramid have? _____

3. How many corners does a rectangular prism have? _____

4. **Reasoning** How are a cube and a rectangular prism alike? How are they different?

_____

_____

_____

_____

_____

PROBLEM-SOLVING STRATEGY
Act It Out

Bricks Jacob wants to know how many bricks there are in the stack, and he knows the stack is completely filled. How many bricks are in the stack?

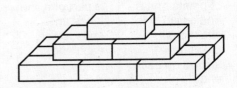

Read and Understand

Step 1: What do you know? The bottom layer of bricks is 3 bricks wide and 3 bricks long. The middle layer of bricks is 2 bricks wide and 2 bricks long. There is one brick on the top.

Step 2: What are you trying to find? The total number of bricks in the stack

Plan and Solve

Step 3: What strategy will you use?   **Strategy:** Act it out

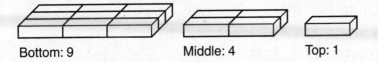

Bottom: 9   Middle: 4   Top: 1

9 + 4 + 1 = 14 Answer: There are a total of 14 bricks in the stack.

Look Back and Check

Step 4: Is your answer reasonable? Yes. The bottom layer has 9, the middle layer has 4, and the top layer has 1 brick.

---

1. When the wall has been built up to the fifth layer, how many cylinder-shaped blocks will have been used?

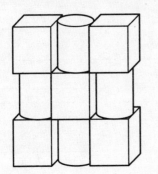

Lines and Line Segments

You can find lines and parts of lines in shapes and objects.

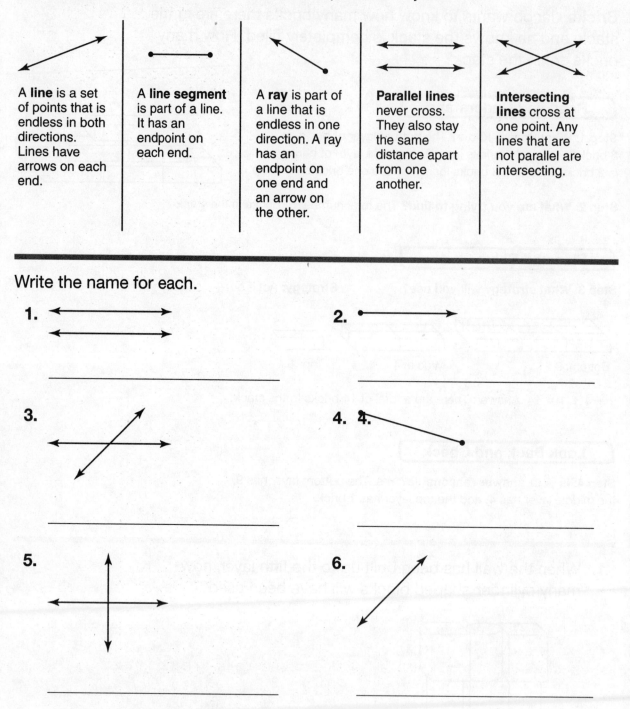

A **line** is a set of points that is endless in both directions. Lines have arrows on each end.

A **line segment** is part of a line. It has an endpoint on each end.

A **ray** is part of a line that is endless in one direction. A ray has an endpoint on one end and an arrow on the other.

Parallel lines never cross. They also stay the same distance apart from one another.

Intersecting lines cross at one point. Any lines that are not parallel are intersecting.

Write the name for each.

1. ←————————→
   ←————————→

   _____

2. •————————→

   _____

3.

   _____

4. 4.

   _____

5.

   _____

6.

   _____

7. **Reasoning** Is it possible for two rays to be parallel to each other? _____

Angles

A **right angle** forms what is normally called a square corner. When two lines form right angles, the lines are called **perpendicular lines.**

An **acute angle** is less than a right angle.

An **obtuse angle** is greater than a right angle.

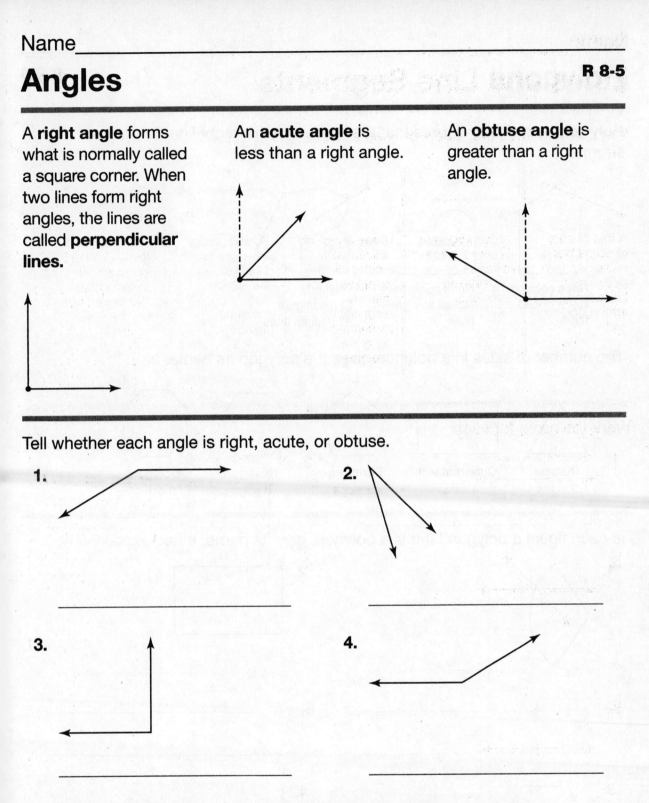

Tell whether each angle is right, acute, or obtuse.

1. _____

2. _____

3. _____

4. _____

Look at the capital letters and tell what kind of angle is in each letter.

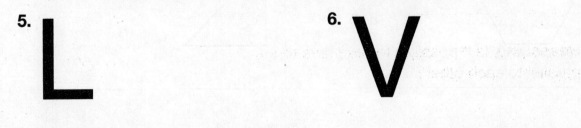

5. **L** _____

6. **V** _____

Name_____

Polygons

R 8-6

Polygons are closed figures that are made up of straight line segments.

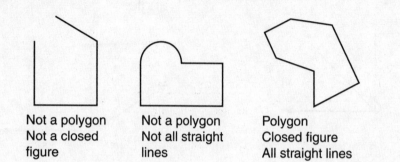

Not a polygon
Not a closed
figure

Not a polygon
Not all straight
lines

Polygon
Closed figure
All straight lines

The number of sides in a polygon gives the polygon its name.

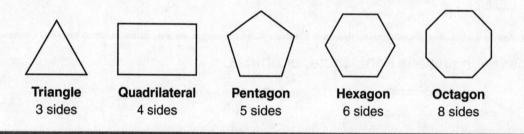

Triangle
3 sides

Quadrilateral
4 sides

Pentagon
5 sides

Hexagon
6 sides

Octagon
8 sides

Is each figure a polygon? If it is a polygon, give its name. If not, explain why.

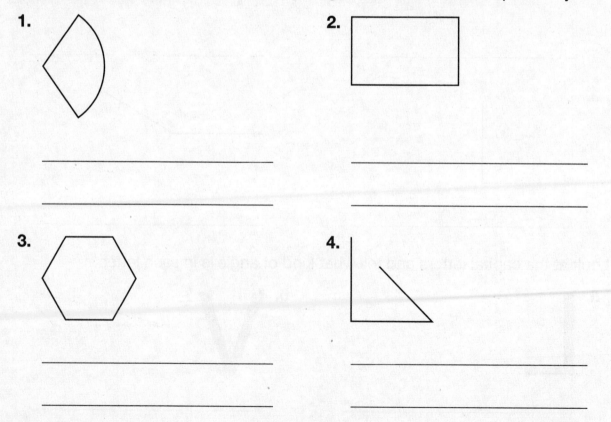

1.

_____

_____

2.

_____

_____

3.

_____

_____

4.

_____

_____

Triangles

Triangles are polygons with three sides.

Triangles can be named by the lengths of their sides.

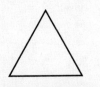 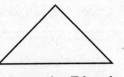 

| **Equilateral Triangle** | **Isosceles Triangle** | **Scalene Triangle** |
| All sides are the same length. | At least two sides are the same length. | No sides are the same length. |

Triangles can also be described by their angles.

| **Right Triangle** | **Acute Triangle** | **Obtuse Triangle** |
| One angle is a right angle. | All three angles are acute angles. | One angle is an obtuse angle. |

Tell if the triangle is equilateral, isosceles, or scalene.

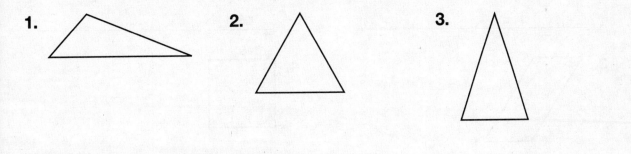

1. _____

2. _____

3. _____

Tell if the triangle is right, acute, or obtuse.

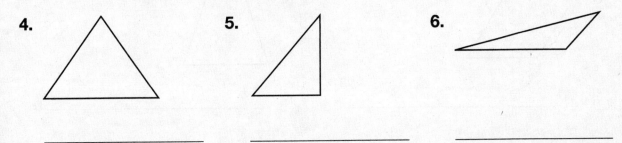

4. _____

5. _____

6. _____

Quadrilaterals

Special quadrilaterals can be separated into groups. The chart shows how they are defined.

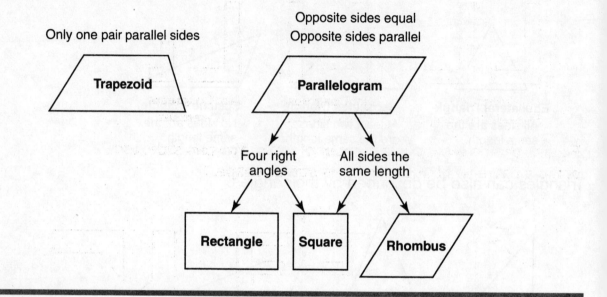

Write the name of each quadrilateral.

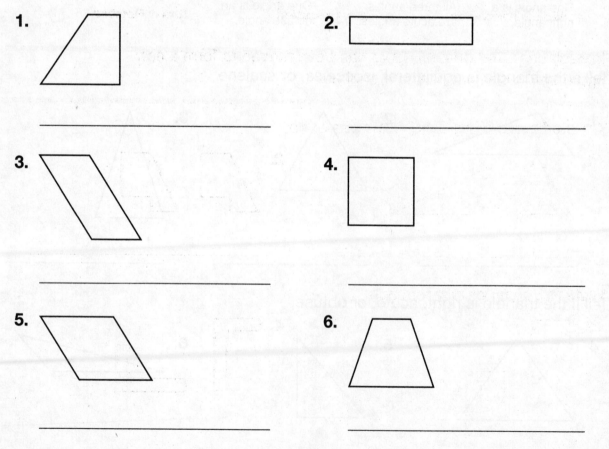

1.

_____

2.

_____

3.

_____

4.

_____

5.

_____

6.

_____

Name_____

Congruent Figures and Motion

Congruent figures are figures that have the same size and the same shape.

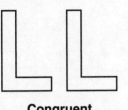

| **Congruent** | **Not Congruent** | **Not Congruent** |
| Same size and shape | Different shape | Different size |

Figures can be moved in a number of ways. You can slide, turn, or flip a figure without changing its size or shape.

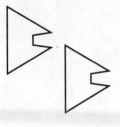 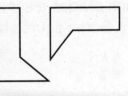

| **Slide** or **Translation** | **Flip** or **Reflection** | **Turn** or **Rotation** |

In each case, the original figure has been moved to form a new figure that is congruent to the original.

Are the figures congruent? Write *yes* or *no*.

1.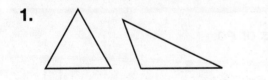

_____

2.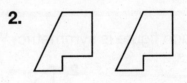

_____

Write *flip*, *slide*, or *turn* for each.

3.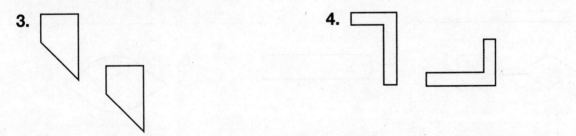

_____

4.

_____

Symmetry

Figures are **symmetric** if you can divide them in half and both halves are congruent.

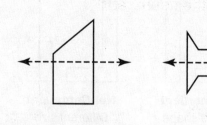

The figure is
symmetric.
The halves match.

The figure is
not symmetric.
The halves do
not match.

The figure is
symmetric.
The halves match.

A line which divides a symmetric figure is called a **line of symmetry.** Some figures have more than one line of symmetry.

The figure
has two lines
of symmetry.

The figure has
one line of
symmetry.

The figure has
three lines of
symmetry.

Tell whether each figure is symmetric. Write *yes* or *no*.

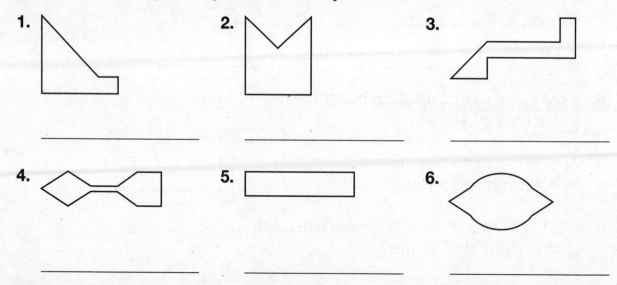

1.

2.

3.

_____   _____   _____

4.

5.

6.

_____   _____   _____

Perimeter

The **perimeter** of a figure is the distance around it.

The perimeter is found by adding the lengths of the sides. To find the perimeter of the figure, add the lengths.

2 ft + 2 ft + 6 ft + 2 ft + 4 ft + 1 ft + 4 ft + 2 ft + 7 ft = 30 ft

The perimeter of the figure is 30 feet.

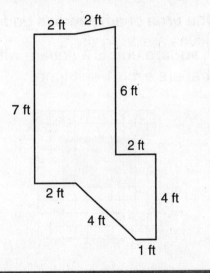

Find the perimeter of each polygon.

1. 4 in. 10 in. 12 in.

2. 4 m 4 m 4 m 2 m 3 m 1 m 1 m 3 m 1 m

_____   _____

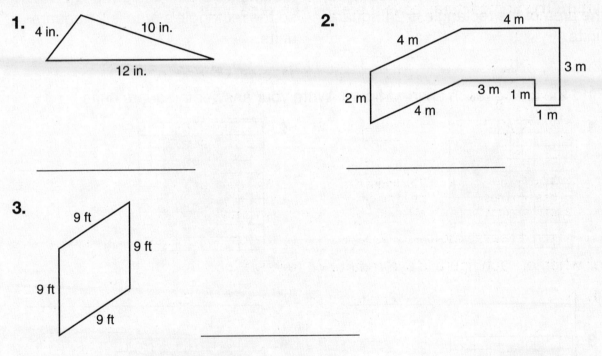

3. 9 ft 9 ft 9 ft 9 ft

_____

4. What is the perimeter of a rectangle that is 5 yd long and 3 yd wide?   _____

5. What is the perimeter of a garden that is 20 ft long and 15 ft wide?   _____

6. What is the perimeter of a square table with a side length of 50 inches?   _____

Name_____

Area

The **area** of a figure can be found in two ways.

A **square unit** is a square with sides that are each 1 unit long.

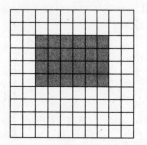

You can think of the grid squares as an array.

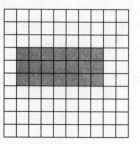

Count the square units in the shaded rectangle. Since there are 24 squares, the area of the rectangle is 24 square units.

Each row has 7 squares. To find the rectangle's area, multiply. $3 \times 7 = 21$, so the rectangle's area is 21 square units.

Find the area of each shaded figure. Write your answer in square units.

1.

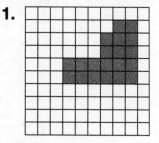

_____

2.

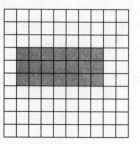

_____

3.

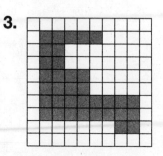

_____

4.

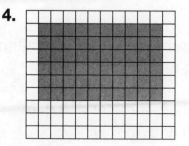

_____

Name_____

Volume

In a solid, the **volume** is the number of cubic units that are
needed to fill the figure. A **cubic unit** is a cube with edges that
are each 1 unit long.

The rectangular prism to the right is
2 units wide, 1 unit high, and 1 unit long.

It takes 2 cubic units to fill the
rectangular prism, so the volume of the
rectangular prism is 2 cubic units.

Find the volume of each figure. Write your answer in cubic units.

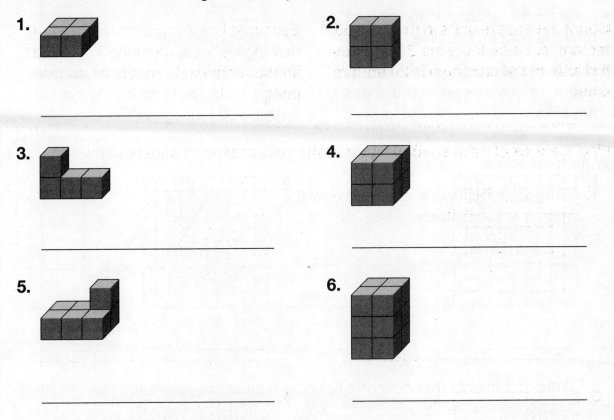

1.

_____

2.

_____

3.

_____

4.

_____

5.

_____

6.

_____

7. **Number Sense** Carl built a cube with edges that
   are 3 in. long. What is the volume of Carl's cube?

_____

Name_____

Polygons Use geometric terms to describe two ways the triangle and the trapezoid are alike.

Tips for writing a good math description:

- Write down all the geometric terms that tell about the shapes in the group.

- Look for the geometric terms that tell how the shapes are alike.

- Use these geometric terms to tell about, or describe, how the shapes are alike.

Example:

Geometric terms that describe how the trapezoid and the triangle are alike:

Right angles

Polygons

Not symmetric

The trapezoid and the triangle both are polygons. They both have a right angle. Neither of them is symmetric.

Write to describe.

1. Write statements that describe how the figures at the right are alike.

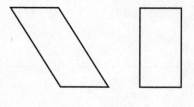

_____

_____

_____

2. Write statements that describe how the figures are different.

_____

_____

_____

Name_____

Kay's New Home

Kay's family has just moved into a new home. Here is a map that shows the house and the land it sits on.

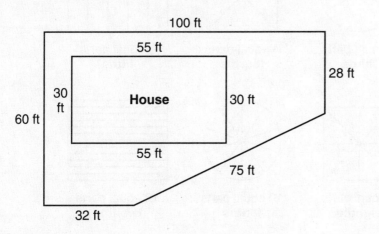

What is the perimeter of the land?

Remember, to find perimeter, add up all of the sides of the figure.

$$100 + 28 + 75 + 32 + 60 = 295 \text{ ft}$$

The land on which Kay's house sits has a perimeter of 295 ft.

---

1. What is the perimeter of Kay's house?   _____

2. Kay's father built a garden in the back yard. What is the area of the garden?

    Garden
    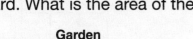

    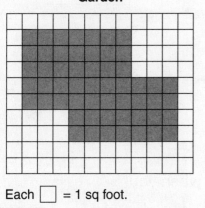

    Each ☐ = 1 sq foot.

3.

    Kay's mother set up a sandbox. What is the shape of the sandbox?

    _____

Name_____

Equal Parts of a Whole

A whole can be divided into equal parts in different ways.

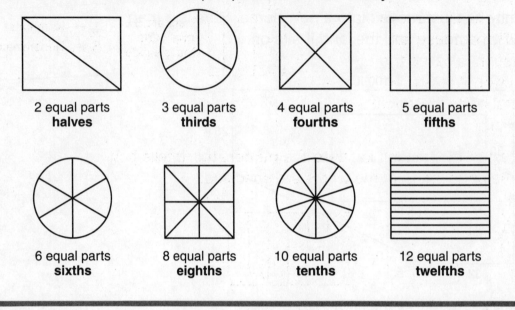

| 2 equal parts **halves** | 3 equal parts **thirds** | 4 equal parts **fourths** | 5 equal parts **fifths** |

| 6 equal parts **sixths** | 8 equal parts **eighths** | 10 equal parts **tenths** | 12 equal parts **twelfths** |

Tell if each shows equal parts or unequal parts.

1. **2.** **3.**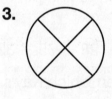

_____   _____   _____

Name the equal parts of the whole.

4. 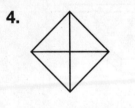   **5.**   **6.**

_____   _____   _____

7. Using grid paper, draw a picture of a whole that is divided into thirds.

8. Reasoning How many equal parts are there when you divide a figure into fifths?   _____

Name_____

Naming Fractional Parts

You can write a fraction to describe the equal parts of a whole. The bottom part of the fraction is called the **denominator**. It tells how many equal parts the whole is divided into.

There are 5 equal parts. One is shaded.

$\dfrac{1}{5}$ ← Numerator
← Denominator

The top part of the fraction is called the **numerator**. It tells how many of the equal parts of the whole are specified.

$\dfrac{2}{3}$ of the circle is shaded.

$\dfrac{1}{2}$ of the square is shaded.

$\dfrac{5}{6}$ of the rectangle is shaded.

Write the fraction of each figure that is shaded.

1.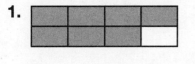

_____

2.

_____

3.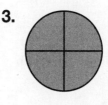

_____

Draw a figure to show each fraction.

4. $\dfrac{1}{3}$

5. $\dfrac{5}{12}$

6. Reasoning A shape is $\dfrac{1}{7}$ shaded. How many parts are not shaded?

_____

Equivalent Fractions

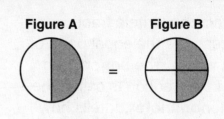

Figure A   **Figure B**

Figure A has 1 out of 2 parts shaded.
The fraction which is shaded is $\frac{1}{2}$.

Figure B has 2 out of 4 parts shaded.
The fraction which is shaded is $\frac{2}{4}$.

Both figures have the same amount shaded. This
means that the fractions $\frac{1}{2}$ and $\frac{2}{4}$ are equivalent.
They both state that half of the figure is shaded.

So, $\frac{2}{4} = \frac{1}{2}$.

Complete each number sentence.

1.

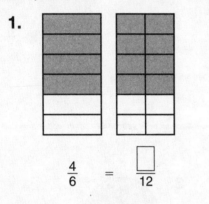

$$\frac{4}{6} = \frac{\boxed{}}{12}$$

2.

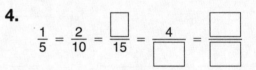

$$\frac{4}{5} = \frac{\boxed{}}{10}$$

Continue each pattern.

3.
$$\frac{1}{3} = \frac{2}{6} = \frac{\boxed{}}{9} = \frac{4}{\boxed{}}$$

4.
$$\frac{1}{5} = \frac{2}{10} = \frac{\boxed{}}{15} = \frac{4}{\boxed{}} = \frac{\boxed{}}{\boxed{}}$$

5. Reasoning Mary and Bill are each reading the same book.
Mary read $\frac{1}{4}$ of the book. Bill says that since he read $\frac{2}{8}$ of
the book, he read more. Is Bill correct? Explain.

_____

_____

_____

Comparing and Ordering Fractions   R 9-4

Compare $\frac{1}{3}$ and $\frac{4}{8}$.

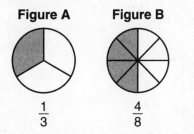

Figure A   Figure B

$\frac{1}{3}$ $\frac{4}{8}$

Both figures are the same size. One
has been divided into thirds, and the
other has been divided into eighths.
You can see that more of Figure B, $\frac{4}{8}$,
is shaded than Figure A, $\frac{1}{3}$. So $\frac{4}{8}$ is
greater than $\frac{1}{3}$.

$\frac{4}{8} > \frac{1}{3}$

Order $\frac{1}{4}$, $\frac{1}{3}$, and $\frac{3}{4}$ from greatest
to least.

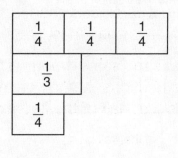

$\frac{3}{4} > \frac{1}{3}$

$\frac{1}{3} > \frac{1}{4}$

So, the fractions in order from greatest
to least are $\frac{3}{4}$, $\frac{1}{3}$, $\frac{1}{4}$.

Compare. Write >, <, or =.

1.

$\frac{1}{5}$ _____ $\frac{2}{6}$

2.

$\frac{6}{8}$ _____ $\frac{3}{4}$

3.

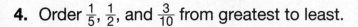

$\frac{7}{12}$ _____ $\frac{4}{6}$

4. Order $\frac{1}{5}$, $\frac{1}{2}$, and $\frac{3}{10}$ from greatest to least.

_____

Name_____

Estimating Fractional Amounts

You can estimate a fractional amount by comparing the amount to fractions you know.

Estimate the fraction of the wall that is painted black.

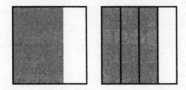

About $\frac{3}{4}$ of the wall is painted black.

Estimate the fraction of the pie that is left.

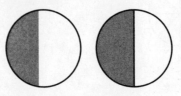

About $\frac{1}{2}$ of the pie is left.

Estimate the amount that is shaded.

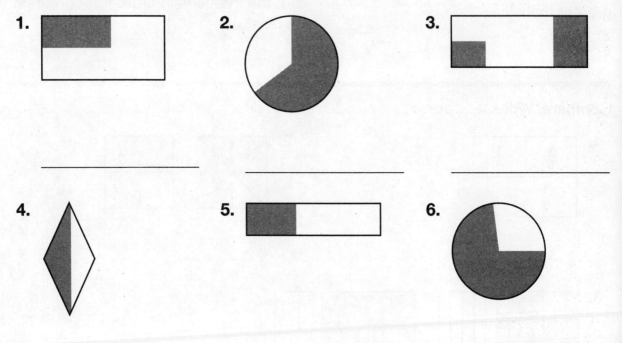

1. _____

2. _____

3. _____

4. _____

5. _____

6. _____

7. **Number Sense** About how much of the casserole is left over?

_____

Fractions on the Number Line

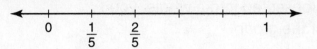

Here is the number line for a denominator of 5, or fifths.

The next two fractions would be $\frac{3}{5}$ and $\frac{4}{5}$.

Write the missing fractions for each number line.

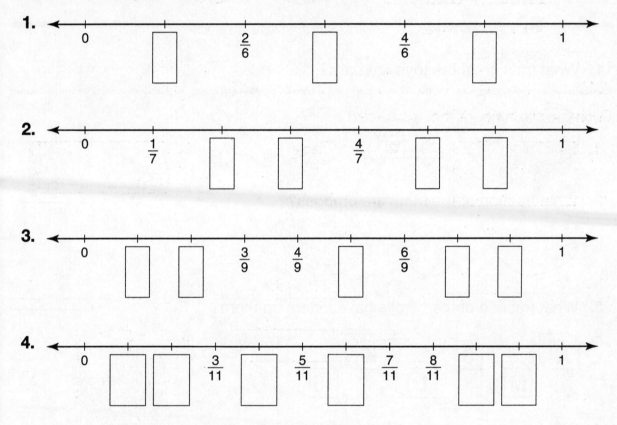

5. **Number Sense** What fraction would come after
   $\frac{5}{8}$ on a number line divided into eighths?   _____

Name_____

Fractions and Sets

R 9-7

When a group of individual items is collected into a whole, you can use a fraction to name a part of the group.

What fraction of the marbles are black?

● ● ● ○ $\dfrac{3}{8}$ ← Number of black marbles
○ ○ ○ ○   ← Total number of marbles

$\dfrac{3}{8}$ of the marbles are black.

---

1. What fraction of the toys are balls?   _____

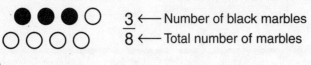

2. What fraction of the fruits are oranges?   _____

3. What fraction of the blocks have letters on them?   _____

4. What fraction of the days of the week begin with the letter *T*?   _____

Draw a picture to show each fraction of a set.

5. $\dfrac{3}{5}$ of the squares are shaded.   **6.** $\dfrac{2}{3}$ of the balls are footballs.

7. Reasoning Out of 6 cats, 2 are tan colored. What fraction of cats are not tan?   _____

118   Use with Lesson 9-7.

Name_____

Finding Fractional Parts of a Set

R 9-8

How to divide to find a fraction of a set:

Find $\frac{1}{3}$ of 15 triangles.

First, divide the 15 triangles into 3 equal groups.

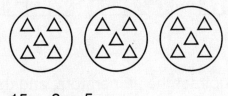

$15 \div 3 = 5$

So, $\frac{1}{3}$ of 15 = 5.

Find $\frac{1}{3}$ of 12 squares.

First, divide the 12 squares into 3 equal groups.

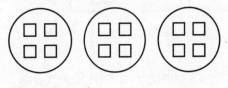

$12 \div 3 = 4$

So, $\frac{1}{3}$ of 12 = 4.

---

1. Find $\frac{1}{2}$ of 10 blocks.

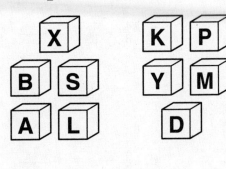

$10 \div 2 =$ _____

$\frac{1}{2}$ of 10 = _____

2. Find $\frac{1}{6}$ of 18 triangles.

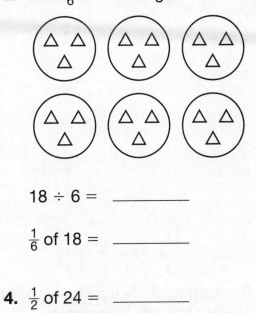

$18 \div 6 =$ _____

$\frac{1}{6}$ of 18 = _____

3. $\frac{1}{3}$ of 9 = _____

4. $\frac{1}{2}$ of 24 = _____

5. $\frac{1}{5}$ of 25 = _____

6. $\frac{1}{4}$ of 40 = _____

7. **Number Sense** When you divide 50 by 2, what fraction of 50 are you finding? Find the answer.

_____

Adding and Subtracting Fractions

Adding fractions:

Find $\frac{2}{4} + \frac{1}{4}$.

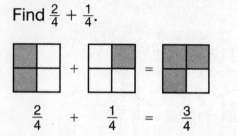

$$\frac{2}{4} \quad + \quad \frac{1}{4} \quad = \quad \frac{3}{4}$$

Add the numerators but keep the denominators the same.

So, $\frac{2}{4} + \frac{1}{4} = \frac{3}{4}$.

Subtracting fractions:

Find $\frac{5}{6} - \frac{4}{6}$.

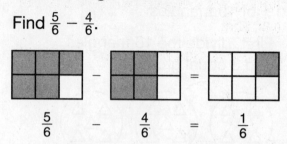

$$\frac{5}{6} \quad - \quad \frac{4}{6} \quad = \quad \frac{1}{6}$$

You subtract the numerators, and the denominator remains the same.

So, $\frac{5}{6} - \frac{4}{6} = \frac{1}{6}$.

Add or subtract. You may use fraction strips or draw a picture to help.

1. $\frac{1}{3} + \frac{1}{3} =$ _____

2. $\frac{3}{5} - \frac{2}{5} =$ _____

3. $\frac{4}{8} + \frac{1}{8} =$ _____

4. $\frac{5}{6} - \frac{2}{6} =$ _____

5. $\frac{10}{12} - \frac{5}{12} =$ _____

6. $\frac{4}{5} - \frac{1}{5} =$ _____

7. Reasoning Judy left $\frac{4}{5}$ of a pot of stew for Dan. Dan ate $\frac{2}{5}$ of what she left. What fraction of the pot of stew was left after Dan ate?

_____

Name_____

Mixed Numbers

A mixed number is a combination of a whole number and a fraction. $5\frac{1}{2}$ is a mixed number. 5 is the whole number, and $\frac{1}{2}$ is the fraction.

How many circles are shown?

How many squares are shown?

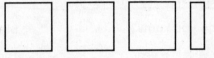

There are 2 whole circles and $\frac{1}{2}$ of another circle.

There are $2\frac{1}{2}$ circles shown.

The mixed number is $2\frac{1}{2}$.

There are 3 whole squares and $\frac{1}{4}$ of another square.

There are $3\frac{1}{4}$ squares shown.

The mixed number is $3\frac{1}{4}$.

Write a mixed number for each picture.

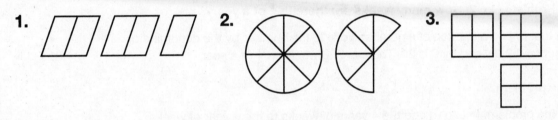

1.

2.

3.

_____   _____   _____

Draw a picture to show each mixed number.

4. $3\frac{2}{5}$

5. $2\frac{1}{3}$

6. **Reasoning** There are 12 doughnuts in a dozen. How many are there in $2\frac{1}{2}$ dozen?

_____

PROBLEM-SOLVING STRATEGY

Solve a Simpler Problem

Weeks How many weeks are there in $4\frac{1}{2}$ years? Remember, there are 52 weeks in a year.

Read and Understand

Step 1: What do you know?

There are 52 weeks in a year.

Step 2: What are you trying to find?

The number of weeks in $4\frac{1}{2}$ years

Plan and Solve

Step 3: What strategy will you use?

Strategy: Solve a simpler problem

Simpler Problem No. 1: How many weeks are there in 4 years?

I know there are 52 weeks in one year. So to find the number of weeks in 4 years, I can multiply 52 × 4, or add 52 + 52 + 52 + 52. There are 208 weeks in 4 years.

Simpler Problem No. 2: How many weeks are there in $\frac{1}{2}$ of a year?

I learned that to find a fraction of a number, I divide the number by the denominator of the fraction. 52 divided by 2 is 26. There are 26 weeks in $\frac{1}{2}$ of a year.

Solve the problem.

To solve the problem, I need to add the 4 years of weeks to the $\frac{1}{2}$ year of weeks. 208 + 26 = 234. So, there are 234 weeks in $4\frac{1}{2}$ years.

Look Back and Check

Step 4: Is your work correct?

Yes. I know that there are close to 50 weeks in a year, and so in 4 years there are close to 200 weeks, and in 5 years there are close to 250 weeks. 234 weeks is close to halfway between 200 and 250.

---

1. Cindy has a pad with 50 pieces of paper in it. Last week she used $\frac{1}{5}$ of the paper. This week she gave 12 sheets of the paper to a friend. How many sheets of paper does Cindy have left?

Length

To use a ruler, line up the object with the 0 mark.

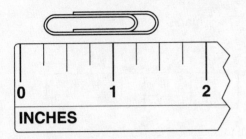

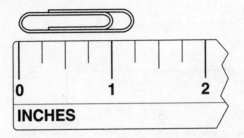

Wrong way. The paper clip is not lined up with the zero.

Right way. By lining the paper clip up with the zero, you can see that it is $1\frac{1}{4}$ inches long, that is 1 inch long to the nearest inch.

Estimate each length. Then measure it to the nearest inch.

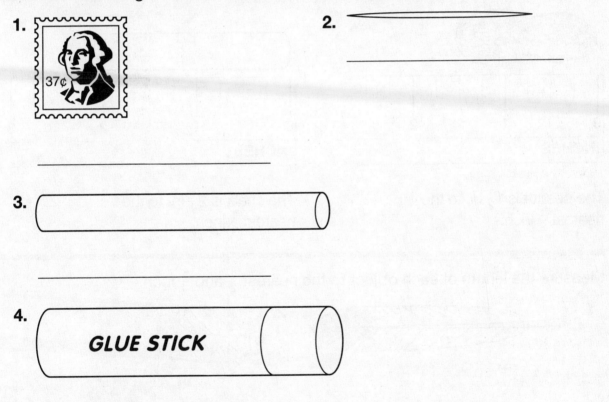

1.

_____

2.

_____

3.

_____

4. GLUE STICK

_____

5. **Number Sense** Estimate the length of one of your index fingers. Then measure. Record the measurement to the nearest inch.

_____

Measuring to the Nearest $\frac{1}{2}$ and $\frac{1}{4}$ Inch

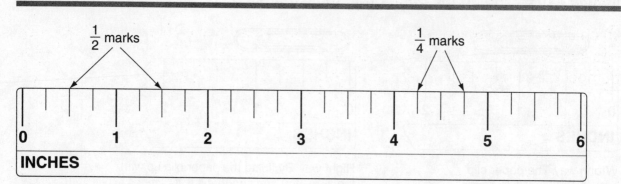

$\frac{1}{2}$ marks $\frac{1}{4}$ marks

INCHES

How long is the peanut to the nearest $\frac{1}{2}$ inch?

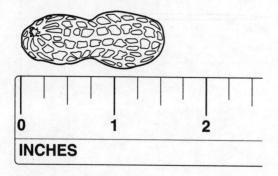

INCHES

The peanut is $1\frac{1}{2}$ in. to the nearest $\frac{1}{2}$ inch.

How long is the chalk to the nearest $\frac{1}{4}$ inch?

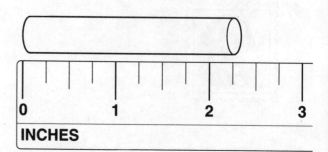

INCHES

The chalk is $2\frac{1}{4}$ in. to the nearest $\frac{1}{4}$ inch.

Measure the length of each object to the nearest $\frac{1}{2}$ and $\frac{1}{4}$ inch.

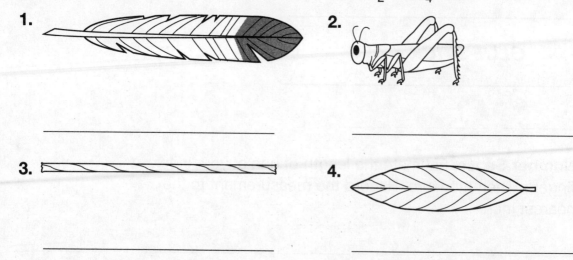

1.

2.

_____

3.

4.

_____

Name_____

Length in Feet and Inches

Longer lengths can be measured in feet. 1 ft is 12 in. long.

To change a measurement from feet into inches, you can multiply the number of feet by 12.

$2 \text{ ft} = \underline{\hspace{2cm}} \text{ in.?}$

$2 \times 12 = 24$

So, 2 ft = 24 in.

How many inches are in 4 ft, 2 in.?

First multiply.

$4 \times 12 \text{ in.} = 48 \text{ in.}$

Then add the extra inches.

48 in. + 2 in. = 50 in.

So, 4 ft, 2 in. = 50 in.

Write each measurement in inches. You may make a table to help.

1. 1 foot, 3 inches

_____

2. 5 feet, 6 inches

_____

3. 2 feet

_____

4. 3 feet, 2 inches

_____

5. 1 foot, 9 inches

_____

6. 6 feet, 3 inches

_____

7. 8 feet

_____

8. 4 feet, 8 inches

_____

9. 7 feet, 7 inches

_____

10. Number Sense Marsha broad jumped 5 ft, 1 in. How many inches did she jump? _____

Name_____

Feet, Yards, and Miles

Customary Units of Length

12 in. = 1 ft

3 ft = 1 yd

36 in. = 1 yd

5,280 ft = 1 mi

1,760 yd = 1 mi

How do you change units?

How many inches are in 4 yd?

Make a table.

Yards	1	2	3	4
Inches	36	72	108	144

There are 144 in. in 4 yd.

How many feet are in 6 yd?

Remember: 1 yd = 3 ft

Multiply.

6×3 ft = 18 ft

There are 18 ft in 6 yd.

Change the units. You may make a table to help.

1. How many feet are in 3 yd?

_____

2. How many inches are in 3 yd?

_____

3. How many feet are in 7 yd?

_____

4. How many feet are in 11 yd?

_____

Compare. Write $<$, $>$, or $=$.

5. 27 in. $\bigcirc$ 2 ft

6. 1 mi $\bigcirc$ 2,000 yd

7. 4 yd $\bigcirc$ 12 in.

8. 72 in. $\bigcirc$ 2 yd

Choose the better estimate.

9. A sleeping bag: 7 ft or 7 yd _____

Name_____

PROBLEM-SOLVING SKILL

R 9-16

Extra or Missing Information

Helmets Henry is working to buy a new bike helmet. The helmet costs $22. Henry makes $5 an hour helping his mother plant flowers. How much has he made so far?

Read and Understand

Step 1: Tell what the question is asking.

How much money has Henry earned so far?

Step 2: Identify key facts and details.

Henry earns $5 per hour. The helmet costs $22.

Plan and Solve

Step 3: Find the extra or missing information.

I do not need to know how much the helmet costs. I do need to know how many hours Henry has worked so far. The problem cannot be solved without knowing the number of hours.

Decide if each problem has extra information or missing information. Solve if you have enough information.

1. There are 3 tables that will be used to serve food at a banquet. The tables are each 6 ft, 2 in. long. How many inches long are the tables if they are put end to end?

_____

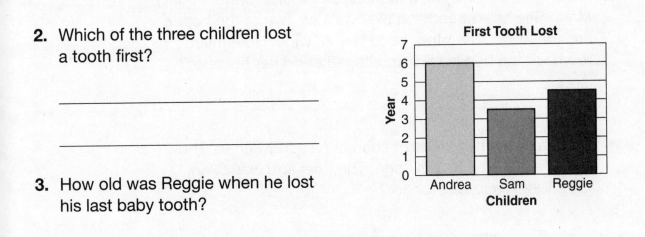

2. Which of the three children lost a tooth first?

_____

_____

3. How old was Reggie when he lost his last baby tooth?

_____

Name_____

The Family Reunion

The Angelo family had a reunion. Over 200 family members from all over the country attended.

Donna Angelo made special pies for the family members to eat. One pie was equally divided into 5 pieces. Bill Angelo ate $\frac{2}{5}$ of the pie. How many pieces were left?

Remember to subtract fractions with the same denominators. First, subtract the numerators. Leave the denominators the same.

$$\frac{5}{5} - \frac{2}{5} = \frac{3}{5}$$

So, 3 pieces of pie were left.

---

1. Diana Angelo is 36 years old. Her son Ted is $\frac{1}{4}$ of her age. How old is Ted?

   _____

2. When George Angelo was born he was 16 in. tall. When he was 10, he was 4 ft, 10 in. tall. As an adult George is 6 ft, 2 in. tall. How many inches did George grow from when he was born until he became an adult? Give your answer in inches.

   _____

3. Heidi Angelo is making a friendship bracelet for her cousin Mara. She has 3 beads on the bracelet. Two of the beads are $\frac{3}{8}$ in. wide. The other bead is $\frac{1}{8}$ in. wide. How much room will the beads take up altogether on her bracelet?

   _____

4. The family ate two kinds of submarine sandwiches. The turkey sub was 4 ft, 2 in. long. The beef sub was 53 in. long. Which sub was longer?

   _____

Tenths

Tenths show 10 equal parts of a whole. Fractions and decimals
can be used to write tenths.

Fractions and decimals:

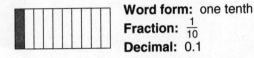

Word form: one tenth
Fraction: $\frac{1}{10}$
Decimal: 0.1

Mixed numbers and decimals:

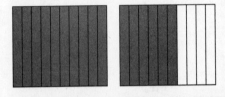

Word form: one and six tenths
Fraction: $1\frac{6}{10}$
Decimal: 1.6

Write a fraction and a decimal for each shaded part.

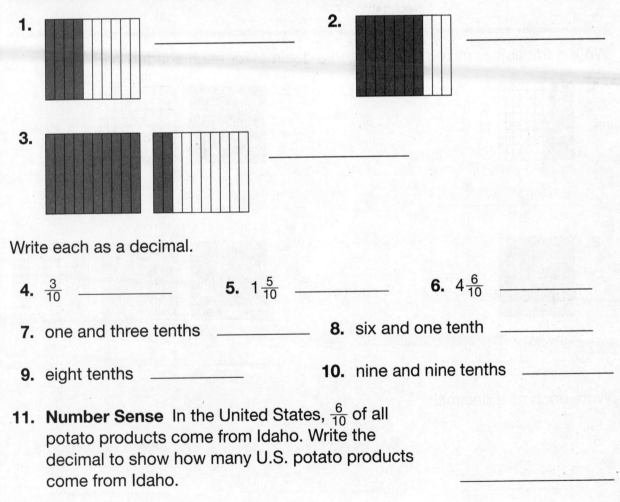

1. _____

2. _____

3. _____

Write each as a decimal.

4. $\frac{3}{10}$ _____

5. $1\frac{5}{10}$ _____

6. $4\frac{6}{10}$ _____

7. one and three tenths _____

8. six and one tenth _____

9. eight tenths _____

10. nine and nine tenths _____

11. **Number Sense** In the United States, $\frac{6}{10}$ of all
potato products come from Idaho. Write the
decimal to show how many U.S. potato products
come from Idaho.

_____

Name_____

Hundredths

Writing hundredths as fractions:

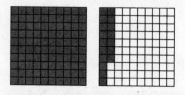

There are 100 squares.
Each square is one hundredth.
53 squares are shaded.
Word form: fifty-three hundredths
Fraction: $\frac{53}{100}$
Decimal: 0.53

Writing hundredths as mixed numbers:

In the left hand grid,
100 out of 100 squares
have been shaded. This
is one whole, or 1.
Word form: one and seventeen
         hundredths
Fraction: $1\frac{17}{100}$
Decimal: 1.17

Write a fraction or mixed number and a decimal for each shaded part.

1.

_____

2.

_____

3.

_____

4.

_____

Write each as a decimal.

5. $\frac{62}{100}$

_____

6. $1\frac{97}{100}$

_____

7. seven hundredths

_____

Comparing and Ordering Decimals

You can use hundreds grids
to compare decimals.

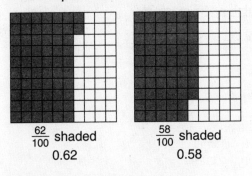

$\frac{62}{100}$ shaded
0.62

$\frac{58}{100}$ shaded
0.58

There are more squares shaded
in 0.62 than in 0.58, so
0.62 is greater.
0.62 > 0.58

You can use number lines to order
decimals.

Order 0.22, 0.13, and 0.37 from least to
greatest.

```
        0.13   0.22        0.37
◄┼───────●──────●──────────●──►
   0    0.10   0.20   0.30  0.40
```

Place the numbers on the number line.
The number that is the farthest right is
the greatest. The number that is the
farthest left is the least.

0.13 < 0.22 < 0.37

So, the numbers in order from least to
greatest are 0.13, 0.22, and 0.37.

Compare. Use <, >, or =.

1.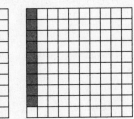

0.10 ◯ 0.09

Use the number line to order the numbers from least to greatest.

```
◄┼───┼────┼────┼────┼────┼────┼────┼────►
 0  0.05 0.10 0.15 0.20 0.25 0.30 0.35 0.40
```

2. 0.22   0.27   0.19   _____

3. 0.04   0.40   0.21   _____

Name_____

Adding and Subtracting Decimals

R 10-4

You can use what you know about adding and subtracting
whole numbers to add and subtract decimals. Just remember
to line up the decimal points before adding or subtracting, and
to place the decimal point in the answer.

Find 8.21 + 5.89.

Step 1	**Step 2**	**Step 3**	**Step 4**
Line up the decimal points.	Add the hundredths.	Add the tenths.	Add the ones. Write a decimal point in the sum.
$\begin{array}{r} 8.21 \\ + 5.89 \\ \hline \end{array}$	$\begin{array}{r} \overset{1}{8.21} \\ + 5.89 \\ \hline 0 \end{array}$	$\begin{array}{r} \overset{1}{8}.\overset{1}{2}1 \\ + 5.89 \\ \hline 10 \end{array}$	$\begin{array}{r} \overset{1}{8}.\overset{1}{2}1 \\ + 5.89 \\ \hline 14.10 \end{array}$

Find 7.45 − 1.18.

Step 1	**Step 2**	**Step 3**	**Step 4**
Line up the decimal points.	Subtract the hundredths. Regroup if needed.	Subtract the tenths. Regroup if needed.	Subtract the ones. Write a decimal point in the difference.
$\begin{array}{r} 7.45 \\ - 1.18 \\ \hline \end{array}$	$\begin{array}{r} \overset{3\ 15}{7.\cancel{45}} \\ - 1.18 \\ \hline 7 \end{array}$	$\begin{array}{r} \overset{3\ 15}{7.\cancel{45}} \\ - 1.18 \\ \hline 27 \end{array}$	$\begin{array}{r} \overset{3\ 15}{7.\cancel{45}} \\ - 1.18 \\ \hline 6.27 \end{array}$

Add.

1. $\begin{array}{r} 3.4 \\ + 6.2 \\ \hline \end{array}$

2. $\begin{array}{r} 0.47 \\ + 1.61 \\ \hline \end{array}$

3. $\begin{array}{r} 7.1 \\ + 4.8 \\ \hline \end{array}$

4. $\begin{array}{r} 2.50 \\ + 1.23 \\ \hline \end{array}$

Subtract.

5. $\begin{array}{r} 5.7 \\ - 2.3 \\ \hline \end{array}$

6. $\begin{array}{r} 7.92 \\ - 5.18 \\ \hline \end{array}$

7. $\begin{array}{r} 9.6 \\ - 5.4 \\ \hline \end{array}$

8. $\begin{array}{r} 1.56 \\ - 1.02 \\ \hline \end{array}$

9. Terry has $1.46 and Cindy has $1.64. How
   much money do they have altogether?   _____

132 Use with Lesson 10-4.

Name_____

Make an Organized List

Posters Lisa has three posters that she would like to put on her door, but only two will fit, one above the other. One is green, one is red, and one is blue. How many different ways can she arrange the two posters on her door?

Read and Understand

Step 1: What do you know?

Two posters will fit on the door. Lisa has three posters. One poster will be above the other.

Step 2: What are you trying to find?

The number of ways two of the posters can be arranged on Lisa's door

Plan and Solve

Step 3: What strategy will you use?

Strategy: Make an organized list

B   B   R   R   G   G

R   G   B   G   B   R

There are 6 ways the posters can be arranged.

Look Back and Check

Step 4: Is your work correct?

Yes; there are no repeats, and all of the posters have been in the top position with each of the others, and the bottom position with each of the others.

Solve. Write the answer in a complete sentence.

1. Jenna, Mac, and Emily are having their picture taken for the yearbook. How many different ways can they line up in a straight line for the picture?

_____

_____

Name_____

Centimeters and Decimeters

A centimeter (cm) is a unit of measurement that is used to measure small objects. A decimeter (dm) is 10 cm long.

1 dm = 10 cm

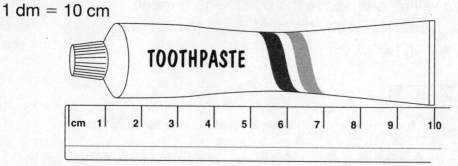

The tube of toothpaste is 10 cm long. We can also say that it is 1 dm long. The cap of the tube is about 1 cm long.

Estimate each length. Then measure to the nearest centimeter.

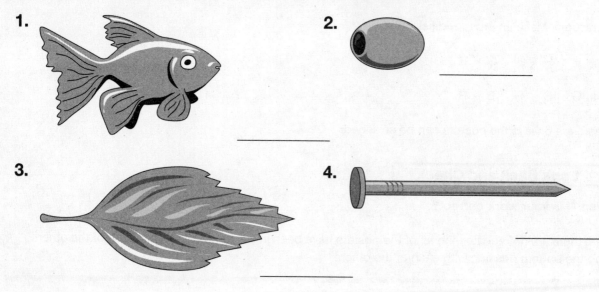

1.

_____

2.

_____

3.

_____

4.

_____

5. **Number Sense** Estimate the length of your leg in centimeters. Then check your estimate.

_____

6. **Writing in Math** Kent says that half of a decimeter is about 3 cm. Do you agree? Explain.

_____

_____

Name_____

Meters and Kilometers

A meter is 100 cm. A kilometer is 1,000 m.

• Centimeters, meters, and kilometers are the most commonly used metric measurements for length or distance.

• Centimeters are used to measure small items, like pencils and paper clips.

• Meters are used to measure larger items, like pieces of lumber. They are also used to measure small distances, such as the distance from the house to the garage.

• Kilometers are used to measure long distances, such as the distance between two towns.

Choose the best estimate for each.

1. the length of a truck _____   **A.** 4 cm

2. a screw _____   **B.** 4 m

3. a bike trail _____   **C.** 4 km

Tell if you would use meters or kilometers for each.

4. the distance to the next door neighbor's house   _____

5. the perimeter of a basketball court   _____

6. the length of a road   _____

7. the length of a playground   _____

8. the distance from Seattle to Chicago   _____

Complete. Use patterns to find the missing numbers.

9.

m	10,000	7,000	5,000	1,000
km			1	

10. **Number Sense** If you drove 8,000 m, how many kilometers did you drive?   _____

Name_____

Writing to Describe

Weight Lifting Barry lifts weights. Use the pattern to complete the table for Days 7 and 8.

Day	1	2	3	4	5	6	7	8
Amount lifted	80 lb	80 lb	85 lb	85 lb	90 lb	90 lb	95 lb	95 lb

Explain how the amount of weight Barry lifts changes as the number of days changes.

Tips for Writing a Math Explanation

- First, find a pattern.

- Tell how the pattern changes the number for each day.

- Use specific numbers as part of your explanation.

- Use words such as *increased* or *decreased*.

Barry lifted the same amount of weight for 2 days in a row, then increased the weight by 5 lb.

As each day increases by 1, the number of pounds either stays the same or increases by 5 lb.

On Day 7 Barry will lift 95 lb because when he increases the weight, he does so by 5 lb: 90 lb + 5 lb = 95 lb.

Because Barry keeps the weight the same for 2 days in a row, he will also lift 95 lb on Day 8.

1. Mary wraps gifts at a department store. She places 3 bows on each gift. Complete the table below to show how many bows she will need to wrap 5 and 6 gifts.

Number of Gifts	1	2	3	4	5	6
Bows	3	6	9	12		

Explain how the number of bows changes as the number of gifts changes.

_____

Name_____

Gudren's Quilts

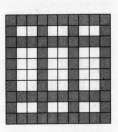

Gudren sews quilts. The quilt she is currently sewing is made of 100 pieces of fabric. Each piece is the same size. How many dark pieces of fabric will she need? Write a fraction and a decimal for the shaded part of the quilt.

There are 64 dark pieces of fabric.

There are 100 squares, and 64 are shaded. So, sixty-four hundredths are shaded.

Fraction: $\frac{64}{100}$ Decimal: 0.64

---

1. How many dark pieces of fabric will Gudren need for the quilt at the right? Write a fraction and a decimal for the shaded part.

2. Gudren is deciding which rectangles to use for her next quilt. She has rectangles that are 0.32 in. long, 0.35 in. long, and 0.23 in. long. Write the lengths in order from least to greatest.

3. Gudren wants to make a quilt for her nephew, who is 5 years old. He loves alligators, so she wants to sew little alligator patches onto the quilt. How many centimeters long is each alligator patch?

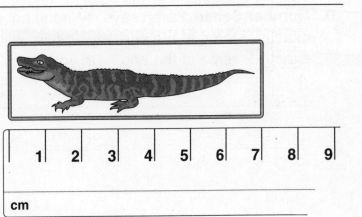

cm

Mental Math: Multiplication Patterns

You can use multiplication patterns to help multiply multiples of 10 and 100.

When one of the factors you are multiplying has zeros on the end, you can multiply the nonzero digits, and then add on the extra zeros.

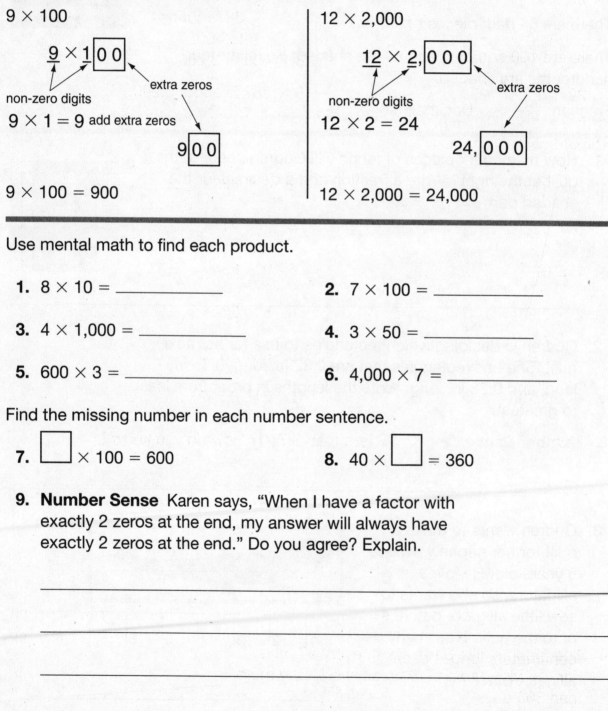

9×100

non-zero digits
extra zeros

$9 \times 1 = 9$ add extra zeros

$9 \times 100 = 900$

$12 \times 2,000$

non-zero digits
extra zeros

$12 \times 2 = 24$

$12 \times 2,000 = 24,000$

Use mental math to find each product.

1. $8 \times 10 = $ _____

2. $7 \times 100 = $ _____

3. $4 \times 1,000 = $ _____

4. $3 \times 50 = $ _____

5. $600 \times 3 = $ _____

6. $4,000 \times 7 = $ _____

Find the missing number in each number sentence.

7. ☐ $\times 100 = 600$

8. $40 \times$ ☐ $= 360$

9. Number Sense Karen says, "When I have a factor with exactly 2 zeros at the end, my answer will always have exactly 2 zeros at the end." Do you agree? Explain.

_____

_____

_____

_____

Name

Estimating Products

You can use rounding to estimate products.

Estimate 6 × 22.

Round 22 to the nearest ten.

6 × 22
    ↓ 22 rounds
      to 20.
6 × 20 = 120

6 × 22 is about 120.

Estimate 8 × 387.

Round 387 to the nearest hundred.

8 × 387
    ↓ 387 rounds
      to 400.
8 × 400 = 3,200

8 × 387 is about 3,200.

Estimate each product.

1. 8 × 91 _____

2. 4 × 689 _____

3. 3 × 53 _____

4. 2 × 2114 _____

5. 7 × 67 _____

6. 9 × 634 _____

7. 8 × 7,984 _____

8. 5 × 362 _____

9. 8 × 5,021 _____

10. 9 × 2,753 _____

11. 6 × 3,103 _____

12. 7 × 8,789 _____

13. Number Sense Is 4 × 857 less than 3,750? How do you know?

_____

_____

_____

14. The Moon orbits Earth about every 27 days.
For the Moon to orbit 9 times, will it take more
than 300 days? _____

Name_____

Mental Math: Division Patterns

R 11-3

When there are zeros at the end of the dividend, you can move them aside and use a basic division fact to divide the nonzero digits.

For example:

$120 \div 4$

$12\boxed{0} \div 4$ ← extra zero

nonzero digits

$12 \div 4 = 3$ add extra zero 30

So, $120 \div 4 = 30$.

Remember to add the same number of zeros back to the quotient that you removed from the dividend.

$6\boxed{0} \div 3 = 2\boxed{0}$ 1 zero

$6\boxed{0\ 0} \div 3 = 2\boxed{0\ 0}$ 2 zeros

$6,\boxed{0\ 0\ 0} \div 3 = 2,\boxed{0\ 0\ 0}$ 3 zeros

Use patterns to find each quotient.

1. $24 \div 4 = $ _____   **2.** $240 \div 4 = $ _____   **3.** $2,400 \div 4 = $ _____

Use mental math to find each quotient.

4. $250 \div 5 = $ _____   **5.** $180 \div 6 = $ _____   **6.** $3,200 \div 8 = $ _____

7. $900 \div 3 = $ _____   **8.** $800 \div 8 = $ _____   **9.** $280 \div 7 = $ _____

10. Number Sense There are 200 school days that are divided into 4 equal grading periods. How many school days are in each grading period?

Name _____

Estimating Quotients

When you know the basic division facts, you can estimate the quotient of a division problem.

Estimate $19 \div 3$.

First, think about the basic facts that you know that use the same divisor, 3.

For example:

$12 \div 3 = 4$ $15 \div 3 = 5$

$18 \div 3 = 6$ $21 \div 3 = 7$

Then choose the basic fact that has the closest dividend to the problem you are solving.

```
          6
• • • • • •
3 • • • • • •
  • • • • • •
```

19 is between the dividends of 18 and 21. It is closer to 18, so use the basic fact $18 \div 3 = 6$.

So, $19 \div 3$ is about 6.

Estimate each quotient.

1. $34 \div 8$ _____

2. $22 \div 3$ _____

3. $46 \div 5$ _____

4. $15 \div 8$ _____

5. $17 \div 6$ _____

6. $58 \div 7$ _____

7. $43 \div 9$ _____

8. $35 \div 4$ _____

9. $74 \div 24$ _____

10. **Reasoning** There are 12 eggs and 5 people. If each person eats the same number of eggs, did each person eat at least 3 eggs? Explain.

_____

_____

_____

Use with Lesson 11-4. **141**

Name_____

Multiplication and Arrays

You can draw a picture of an array to show multiplication.

For example:

4 × 21

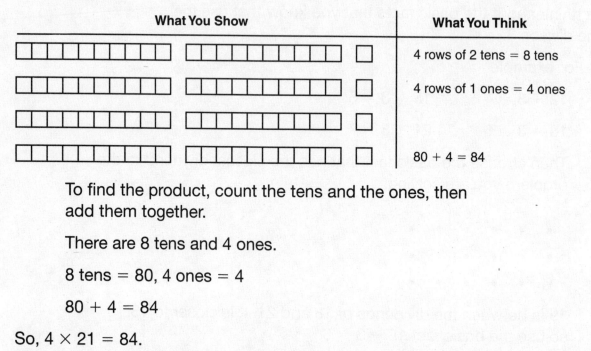

What You Show	What You Think
	4 rows of 2 tens = 8 tens
	4 rows of 1 ones = 4 ones
	80 + 4 = 84

To find the product, count the tens and the ones, then add them together.

There are 8 tens and 4 ones.

8 tens = 80, 4 ones = 4

80 + 4 = 84

So, 4 × 21 = 84.

Find each product. You may draw a picture to help.

1. 3 × 14 = 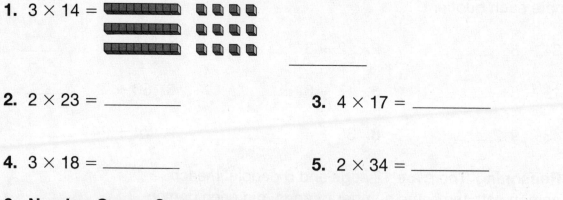 _____

2. 2 × 23 = _____

3. 4 × 17 = _____

4. 3 × 18 = _____

5. 2 × 34 = _____

6. Number Sense Suppose you wanted to draw an array for 21 × 3. How many ones would you draw?

_____

Breaking Numbers Apart to Multiply

You can make multiplication easier by breaking larger numbers apart by place value.

Find 4 × 23.

23 is the same as 20 + 3.

First multiply the ones, then multiply the tens.

4 × 20 = 80   4 × 3 = 12

Then add the products together.   80 + 12 = 92

So, 4 × 23 = 92.

Find each product.

1. 21
     × 6

2. 43
     × 5

3. 16
     × 8

4. $38
     ×   9

5. 62 × 4 = _____

6. 2 × 19 = _____

7. 4 × 22 = _____

8. 5 × 21 = _____

9. Number Sense Tim said, "To find 6 × 33, I can add 18 and 18."
   Do you agree with him? Why or why not?

_____

_____

_____

_____

Name_____

Multiplying Two-Digit Numbers

You can regroup tens and ones to multiply two-digit numbers.

Find 36 × 3.

	What You Think	**What You Write**
Step 1	Multiply the ones. Regroup if necessary. 6 × 3 = 18 ones. Regroup 18 ones as 1 ten 8 ones.	$\begin{array}{r} 1 \\ 36 \\ \times\ \ 3 \\ \hline 8 \end{array}$
Step 2	Multiply the tens. Add any regrouped tens. 3 × 3 tens = 9 tens. 9 tens + 1 ten = 10 tens.	$\begin{array}{r} 1 \\ 36 \\ \times\ \ 3 \\ \hline 108 \end{array}$

So, 36 × 3 = 108.

Find each product. Decide if your answer is reasonable.

1. $\begin{array}{r} 21 \\ \times\ \ 6 \\ \hline \end{array}$

2. $\begin{array}{r} 14 \\ \times\ \ 3 \\ \hline \end{array}$

3. $\begin{array}{r} 32 \\ \times\ \ 4 \\ \hline \end{array}$

4. $\begin{array}{r} 57 \\ \times\ \ 5 \\ \hline \end{array}$

5. $\begin{array}{r} 62 \\ \times\ \ 8 \\ \hline \end{array}$

6. $\begin{array}{r} 33 \\ \times\ \ 5 \\ \hline \end{array}$

7. 43 × 8 = _____

8. 28 × 6 = _____

9. 43 × 2 = _____

10. **Number Sense** The largest snowman on record was almost 38 yd tall. There are 3 ft in a yard. How many feet are in 38 yd?

_____

Multiplying Three-Digit Numbers

A three-digit factor is multiplied the same way a two-digit factor is.

Find 523×7.

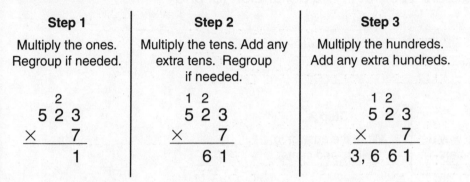

Step 1	Step 2	Step 3
Multiply the ones. Regroup if needed.	Multiply the tens. Add any extra tens. Regroup if needed.	Multiply the hundreds. Add any extra hundreds.

$$\begin{array}{r} 2 \\ 5\,2\,3 \\ \times7 \\ \hline 1 \end{array} \qquad \begin{array}{r} 1\,2 \\ 5\,2\,3 \\ \times7 \\ \hline 6\,1 \end{array} \qquad \begin{array}{r} 1\,2 \\ 5\,2\,3 \\ \times7 \\ \hline 3,6\,6\,1 \end{array}$$

Estimate to check. $523 \times 7 = 500 \times 7 = 3,500$.
3,661 is close to 3,500, so the answer is reasonable.

Remember, it is important to always start with the ones place, and work from the least place value to the greatest. Any regrouping needs to be done going from least to greatest.

Find each answer. Estimate to check reasonableness.

1. $\begin{array}{r} 221 \\ \times4 \\ \hline \end{array}$
2. $\begin{array}{r} 342 \\ \times5 \\ \hline \end{array}$
3. $\begin{array}{r} 402 \\ \times4 \\ \hline \end{array}$

4. $\begin{array}{r} 610 \\ \times2 \\ \hline \end{array}$
5. $\begin{array}{r} 531 \\ \times3 \\ \hline \end{array}$
6. $\begin{array}{r} 213 \\ \times8 \\ \hline \end{array}$

7. $392 \times 6 = $ _____

8. $104 \times 9 = $ _____

9. **Number Sense** The Tonga micro-plate near Samoa moves at a rate of 240 mm each year. At that rate, how many millimeters will the plate have moved in 5 years?

_____

_____

Multiplying Money

The only difference between multiplying money and whole numbers is the final step. The answer must be written in the form of money. Make sure you put in the dollar sign ($) and the decimal point.

For example:

Find $7.36 × 7.

Step 1	Step 2
Multiply the same way as with whole numbers.	Write the answer in dollars and cents.

$$\begin{array}{r} {\scriptstyle 2\ \ 4} \\ \$7\ .\ 3\ 6 \\ \times\qquad 7 \\ \hline 5\ 1\quad 5\ 2 \end{array} \qquad \begin{array}{r} {\scriptstyle 2\ \ 4} \\ \$7\ .\ 3\ 6 \\ \times\qquad 7 \\ \hline \$5\ 1\ .\ 5\ 2 \end{array}$$

Estimate to check. $7 \times \$7.36 = 7 \times 7 = 49$
$51.52 is close to 49, so the answer is reasonable.

Find each product. Estimate to check reasonableness.

1.	$1.25 × 3	2.	$6.98 × 2	3.	$4.24 × 5	4.	$3.42 × 8

5. Kirk bought 3 roast beef sandwiches. How much did it cost?

_____

6. If you bought 7 tuna sandwiches, how much would it cost?

_____

Lunch Menu	
Tuna Sandwich	$4.53
Roast Beef Sandwich	$5.15
Chips	$1.28
Drink	$1.14

7. **Number Sense** Write a multiplication sentence with a 3-digit number that does not require regrouping.

_____

Choose a Computation Method

If the answer is easy to find, you can use mental math. Use mental math for problems like:

$90 \div 9$ or $3,000 \times 7$.

If the answer is not too difficult to find, and there are not many regroupings, use paper and pencil. Use paper and pencil for problems like:

$912 \div 3$ or 62×4 or $615 + 88$.

For problems that have a lot of regroupings, a calculator is a good choice. Some problems that you might choose a calculator to solve are:

$15,328 \times 37$ or $8,921,320 \div 8$.

Find each product. Tell which computation method you used.

1. $\begin{array}{r} 3,000 \\ \times \quad\ 4 \\ \hline \end{array}$

2. $\begin{array}{r} 189 \\ \times \quad 2 \\ \hline \end{array}$

3. $\begin{array}{r} \$302 \\ \times \quad\ 9 \\ \hline \end{array}$

4. $5,887 \times 6 =$ _____

5. $\$421 \times 3 =$ _____

6. $\$500 \times 7 =$ _____

7. Writing in Math Why is mental math not a good method to use when finding $6,789 \times 5$?

_____

_____

_____

PROBLEM-SOLVING STRATEGY   **R 11-11**
Use Logical Reasoning

Age Carla is 18 years old. Her father is 4 years older than her mother. Carla's mother is twice as old as Carla. How old is Carla's father?

Read and Understand

Step 1: What do you know?

Carla's age is 18. Carla's mother is twice Carla's age. Her father is 4 years older than her mother.

Step 2: What are you trying to find?

Carla's father's age

Plan and Solve

Step 3: What strategy will you use?

Strategy: Use logical reasoning

Draw a picture to help organize what you know.

Carla's mother is twice Carla's age, or 2 × 18 = 36. So, Carla's mother is 36. Carla's father is 4 years older than her mother, or 36 + 4 = 40. So, Carla's father is 40 years old.

Look Back and Check

Step 4: Is your work correct?

Yes, all the clues match the answer.

Solve. Write the answer in a complete sentence.

1. Complete the table to decide what color house Peter lives in.

    Clues:
    • Tom does not live in a blue house.
    • Willis likes his white house.

	Peter	Tom	Willis
Blue			
Green			
White			

_____

_____

Name_____

Using Objects to Divide

How to use place-value blocks to show division with greater numbers:

Find 45 ÷ 3.

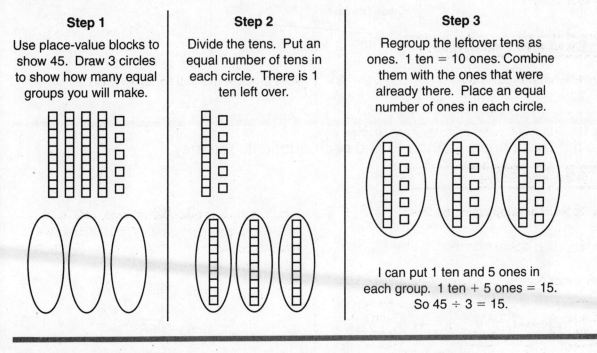

Step 1	**Step 2**	**Step 3**
Use place-value blocks to show 45. Draw 3 circles to show how many equal groups you will make.	Divide the tens. Put an equal number of tens in each circle. There is 1 ten left over.	Regroup the leftover tens as ones. 1 ten = 10 ones. Combine them with the ones that were already there. Place an equal number of ones in each circle.

I can put 1 ten and 5 ones in
each group. 1 ten + 5 ones = 15.
So 45 ÷ 3 = 15.

Use place-value blocks or draw a picture to find each quotient.

1. 46 ÷ 2 = _____

2. 48 ÷ 4 = _____

3. 72 ÷ 3 = _____

4. 39 ÷ 3 = _____

5. 60 ÷ 4 = _____

6. 98 ÷ 7 = _____

7. 88 ÷ 4 = _____

8. 51 ÷ 3 = _____

9. 57 ÷ 3 = _____

10. 96 ÷ 6 = _____

11. Number Sense Tim's mom is packing fruit bars for her
3 sons to take on a campout. She has 36 mini-sized bars.
How many bars will each son have packed?

_____

Breaking Numbers Apart to Divide   R 11-13

You can break apart numbers into groups of tens and ones to divide.

Find 42 ÷ 2.

Step 1 Break apart 42 into tens and ones.	**Step 2** Divide the tens, then divide the ones.	**Step 3** Add the two quotients.
42 is the same as 4 tens and 2 ones.	Tens: 40 ÷ 2 = 20	20 + 1 = 21
42 = 40 + 2	Ones: 2 ÷ 2 = 1	So, 42 ÷ 2 = 21.

Use the break apart method to find each quotient. You may draw a picture to help.

1. 55 ÷ 5 = _____   2. 48 ÷ 4 = _____   3. 82 ÷ 2 = _____

4. 3)93   5. 2)46   6. 3)66

7. 63 ÷ 3 = _____   8. 88 ÷ 4 = _____   9. 24 ÷ 2 = _____

10. 4)44   11. 3)96   12. 6)66

13. **Number Sense** Niko has 28 pencils. He is putting them evenly into two drawers. How many pencils will be in each drawer?

_____

Find 51 ÷ 3.

	What You Think	**What You Write**
Step 1	Divide the tens. 5 tens ÷ 3 = 1 ten with 2 tens left over.	1 ← 1 ten in each group 3)51 −3 ← (3 × 1) tens used 2 ← 2 tens left over
Step 2	Regroup the tens as ones. 2 tens = 20 ones. Combine with the 1 one already there.	1 3)51 −3↓ Bring down the 1 one. 21 21 ones in all
Step 3	Divide the ones.	17 ← 17 ones in each group 3)51 −3 21 −21 ← (7 × 3) ones used 0 ← 0 ones left over

Complete. Check your answer.

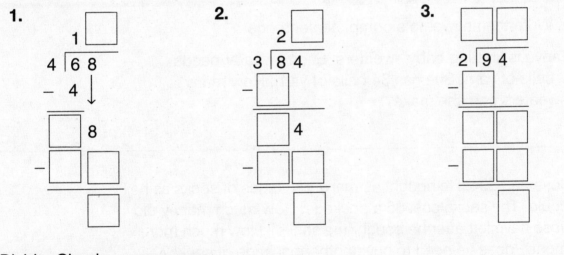

1.

```
     1 □
  4 )6 8
   − 4 ↓
   ┌─┐
   │ │ 8
   └─┘
 −□ □
   ┌─┐
   │ │
   └─┘
```

2.

```
     2 □
  3 )8 4
   −□
   □ □
     4
 −□ □
   ┌─┐
   │ │
   └─┘
```

3.

```
   □ □
  2 )9 4
  −□
  □ □
 −□ □
   ┌─┐
   │ │
   └─┘
```

Divide. Check your answers.

4. 73 ÷ 2 = _____   **5.** 63 ÷ 3 = _____   **6.** 96 ÷ 8 = _____

7. Number Sense If you divide 20 ÷ 5, will there be a remainder?
How do you know?

_____

_____

PROBLEM-SOLVING SKILL
Interpreting Remainders

Window Repair Sam repairs broken windows. It takes him about 4 hr to repair 1 window. He works 25 hr each week.

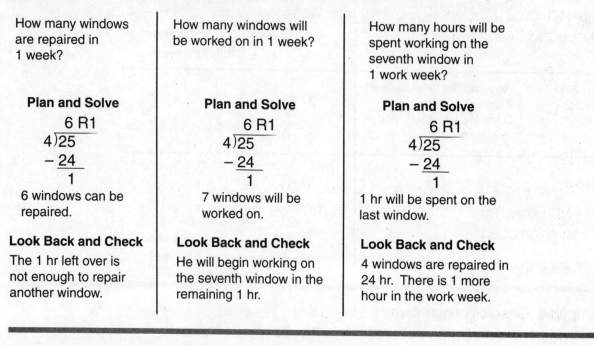

How many windows are repaired in 1 week?

Plan and Solve

```
    6 R1
4)25
  -24
    1
```

6 windows can be repaired.

Look Back and Check

The 1 hr left over is not enough to repair another window.

How many windows will be worked on in 1 week?

Plan and Solve

```
    6 R1
4)25
  -24
    1
```

7 windows will be worked on.

Look Back and Check

He will begin working on the seventh window in the remaining 1 hr.

How many hours will be spent working on the seventh window in 1 work week?

Plan and Solve

```
    6 R1
4)25
  -24
    1
```

1 hr will be spent on the last window.

Look Back and Check

4 windows are repaired in 24 hr. There is 1 more hour in the work week.

Solve. Write the answer in a complete sentence.

1. Tanya is knitting baby sweaters. Each sweater needs 5 balls of yarn. She has 34 balls of yarn. How many sweaters can she make?

_____

2. José had $34. He bought as many packages of socks as he could. The socks cost $5 a package. How much money did José have left after he bought the socks? How much more money does he need to buy another package of socks?

_____

_____

Name_____

The Volleyball Team

Volleyball Team The elementary school has just started a
volleyball team, and 42 girls signed up. They would like to have
at least 1 coach for every 8 girls. How many volleyball coaches
are needed?

$$\begin{array}{r} 5 \\ 8\overline{)42} \\ -40 \\ \hline 2 \end{array}$$

$42 \div 8 = 5$ R2

There are 2 girls left without a coach. So I need to have at
least one more coach if I want to have no more than 8 girls
to each coach.

So, 6 coaches are needed.

1. Lydia is buying caps for the girls on her volleyball
   squad. The caps cost $3.99 each. There are
   7 girls on Lydia's squad. How much will Lydia spend? _____

2. Sara, Cheryl, and Joan each have a different-colored shirt
   on. Their shirts are red, blue, and pink. Cheryl is not wearing
   pink, and Sara is wearing red. What color is Joan's shirt?

   _____

3. There are 4 rows left in the auditorium. Each row has
   18 seats in it. There are 3 classes that still need to be
   seated. There are 23, 27, and 24 students in the classes.
   Will there be enough seats?

   _____

4. A team is having an end-of-season party at a local
   restaurant. There are 19 people coming, and the tables
   each seat 4. How many tables do they need to reserve?

   _____

Name_____

Customary Units of Capacity

Capacity is the amount of liquid a container can hold. The customary system measures capacity in cups, pints, quarts, and gallons, from smallest to largest.

    2 cups (c) = 1 pint (pt)

    2 pints (pt) = 1 quart (qt)

    4 quarts (qt) = 1 gallon (gal)

4 gal = _____ qt

You are going from a large unit (gallons) to a smaller unit (quarts), so you are going to use multiplication. There are 4 qt in 1 gal.

Multiply the number of gallons by 4 to find the number of quarts.

    4 gal × 4 = 16

    4 gal = 16 qt

6 c = _____ pt

You are going from a smaller unit (cups) to a larger unit (pints), so you are going to use division.

There are 2 c in 1 pt.

Divide the number of cups by 2 to find the number of pints.

    6 c ÷ 2 = 3

    6 c = 3 pt

Estimate Choose the better estimate for each.

1. 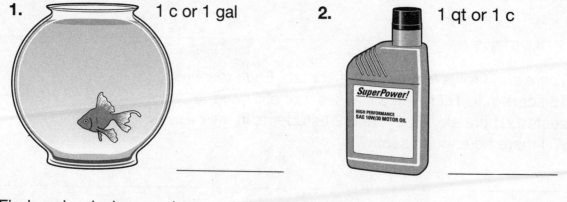 1 c or 1 gal

_____

2. 1 qt or 1 c

_____

Find each missing number.

3. 3 gal = _____ qt   **4.** 4 pt = _____ qt   **5.** 4 pt = _____ c

6. 5 qt = _____ pt   **7.** 10 c = _____ pt   **8.** 20 qt = _____ gal

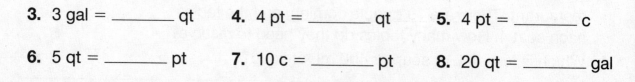

Name_____

Milliliters and Liters

Milliliters (mL) are commonly used to measure very small amounts of liquid. There are 5 mL in 1 tsp.

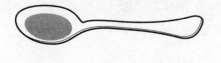

A liter is a little more than 1 qt. 1 L = 1,000 mL. Many beverages, such as sports drinks, spring water, and soda, are packaged in 1 or 2 L bottles.

How to change between liters and milliliters:

7,000 mL = _____ L

You know that 1,000 mL = 1 L, so 7,000 mL = 7 × 1 L.

7,000 mL = 7 L

8 L = _____ mL

You know that 1 L = 1,000 mL, so 8 L = 8 × 1,000 mL.

8 L = 8,000 mL

Estimation Choose the better estimate for each.

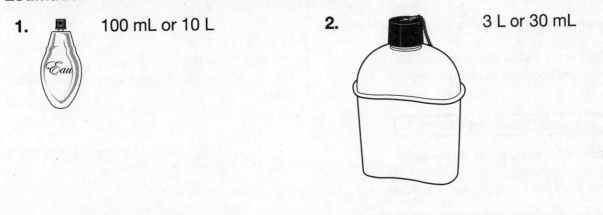

1. 100 mL or 10 L

_____

2. 3 L or 30 mL

_____

3. Which is more, 2,500 mL of milk or 3 L of milk?

_____

4. Which is less, 4 L of soup or 400 mL of soup?

_____

Name_____

Work Backward

Larry's Dog When Larry was in fourth grade, his dog gained 7 lb. The dog was sick over the summer and lost 3 lb. When Larry started fifth grade, his dog weighed 81 lb. How much did Larry's dog weigh when Larry started fourth grade?

Read and Understand

Step 1: What do you know?

The dog weighed 81 lb when Larry started fifth grade. The dog gained 7 lb when Larry was in fourth grade, and lost 3 lb over the summer.

Step 2: What are you trying to find?

How much Larry's dog weighed when Larry started fourth grade

Plan and Solve

Step 3: What strategy will you use?

Strategy: Work backward

Draw a picture to show each change.

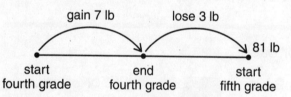

Start at the end, work backward using the opposite operation of each change.

Where the dog gained weight, I subtract. Where the dog lost weight, I add.

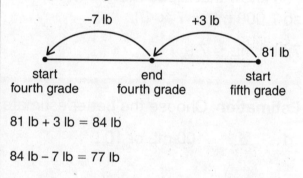

81 lb + 3 lb = 84 lb

84 lb − 7 lb = 77 lb

The dog weighed 77 lb when Larry started fourth grade.

Look Back and Check

Step 4: Is your answer reasonable?

Yes, I worked backward using the weights that were known.

---

1. Cristie spent $6.50 on food and $22.50 on a haircut. She had $5.00 left. How much money did she have before she spent any?

_____

_____

Customary Units of Weight

The reference book weighs 3 lb. How many ounces is that?

3 lb = _____ oz

1 lb = 16 oz

3 × 16 oz = 48 oz

3 lb = 48 oz

So, the reference book weighs 48 oz.

23 oz = _____ lb

Think of 23 oz as 16 oz + 7 oz.

Then you can replace 16 oz with 1 lb.

23 oz = 16 oz + 7 oz

23 oz = 1 lb 7 oz

So, 23 oz = 1 lb 7 oz.

Choose the better estimate for each weight.

1. banana
8 oz or 8 lb

_____

2. car
1,000 lb or 1,000 oz

_____

3. egg
1 oz or 1 lb

_____

4. cat
10 lb or 10 oz

_____

Find each missing number.

5. 5 lb = _____ oz

6. 19 oz = _____ 1 lb _____ oz

7. 2 lb 3 oz = _____ oz

8. 37 oz = _____ lb _____ oz

9. 10 lb = _____ oz

10. 1 lb 5 oz = _____ oz

11. Number Sense Which is greater, 161 oz or 10 lb?

_____

Grams and Kilograms

Grams and kilograms are the metric units to tell how heavy
an object is. 1 kg is equal to 1,000 g. A gram is about as
heavy as a paper clip.

How to change between grams and kilograms:

To convert from kilograms to grams, you multiply by 1,000.	To convert from grams to kilograms, you divide by 1,000.
2 kg = _____ g	4,000 g = _____ kg
1 kg = 1,000 g, so 2 kg = 2 × 1,000 g	4,000 g ÷ 1,000 = 4 kg
2 kg = 2,000 g	4,000 g = 4 kg

Choose the better estimate for each.

1. 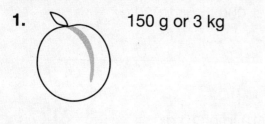   150 g or 3 kg

_____

2. 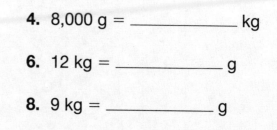   1 kg or 1 g

_____

Find each missing number.

3. 5 kg = _____ g   **4.** 8,000 g = _____ kg

5. 6 kg = _____ g   **6.** 12 kg = _____ g

7. 7,000 g = _____ kg   **8.** 9 kg = _____ g

Temperature

On the Fahrenheit scale, water freezes at 32°F and boils at 212°F. At 32°F you would need a winter parka, gloves, and a warm hat if you were planning to go outdoors.

On the Celsius scale, water boils at 100°C and freezes at 0°C. At 32°C, you would wear shorts and a T-shirt.

How to read a thermometer

The top of the column is at 80 on the Fahrenheit scale, so the temperature is 80°F. The top of the column is at about 28 on the Celsius scale, so the temperature is about 28°C.

Write each temperature using °C.

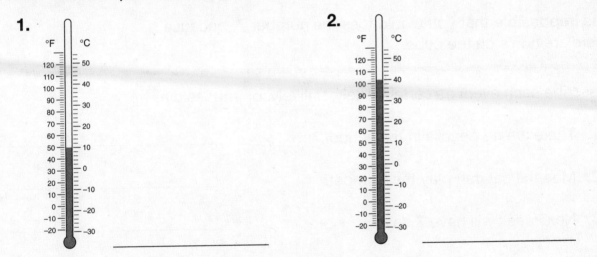

1.

2.

Write each temperature using °F.

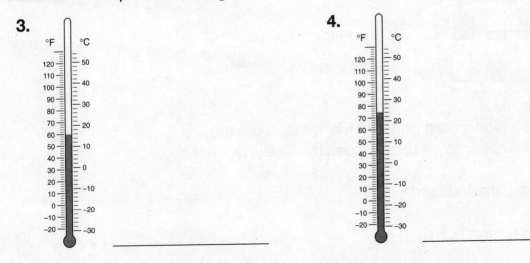

3.

4.

Describing Chance

You can use the words **certain**, **likely**, **unlikely**, or **impossible** to describe the chance that something will happen.

If you were to toss the number cube to the right:

It is **certain** that you would toss a number from 1 to 6, because all of the numbers are between 1 and 6.

It is **likely** that you would toss a number greater than 1. There are 5 numbers that are greater than 1, and there is 1 number that is not greater than 1.

It is **unlikely** that you will toss a 6. There are 5 numbers that are not 6, and one number that is 6. The event does not have a good chance of happening, but it could.

It is **impossible** that you would toss the number 7, because there are no 7s on the cube.

Describe each event as certain, likely, unlikely, or impossible.

1. There are no pencils in the school. _____

2. Moe the cat can play the trumpet. _____

3. Next week will have 7 days. _____

4. Janet's dog has 4 legs. _____

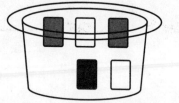

Suppose you pick a card from the hat without looking.
Describe each pick as certain, impossible, likely, or unlikely.

5. Picking a shaded card _____

6. Picking a round card _____

7. Picking a card that is not a black card _____

Name _____

Fair and Unfair

R 12-8

Spinner X

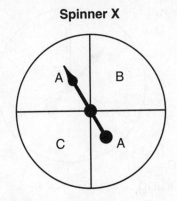

Spinner Y

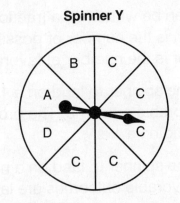

Spinner X has 4 sections.

There is a 1 out of 4 chance that Spinner X will land on the letter B.

There is a 2 out of 4 chance that Spinner X will land on the letter A.

Spinner Y has 8 sections.

There is a 1 out of 8 chance that Spinner Y will land on the letter A.

There is a 5 out of 8 chance that Spinner Y will land on the letter C.

Give the chance of each outcome.

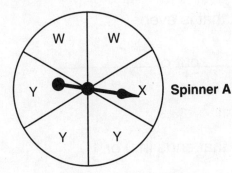

Spinner A

1. the letter W _____ out of _____

2. the letter Y _____ out of _____

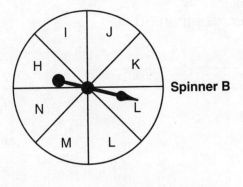

Spinner B

3. the letter H _____ out of _____

4. the letter L _____ out of _____

Use with Lesson 12-8. **161**

Probability

Probability can be written as a fraction. The denominator of the fraction is the number of possible outcomes and the numerator is the number of favorable outcomes.

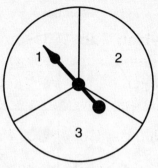

If you want the spinner to land on a 1, then landing on a 1 is the favorable outcome. The probability of the spinner landing on a 1 is $\frac{1}{3}$.

If you want the spinner to land on a number greater than 1, then the favorable outcomes are landing on a 2 or landing on a 3.

The chance of landing on a number greater than 1 is 2 out of 3.

The probability of the spinner landing on a number greater than 1 is $\frac{2}{3}$.

A number cube has the numbers 10, 20, 30, 45, 51, and 60 on its sides.

Give the chance and probability of each event.

1. Tossing a number that is even

Chance: _____ out of _____

Probability: $\dfrac{\boxed{}}{6}$

2. Tossing a number that ends in 0 or 1

Chance: _____ out of _____

Probability: $\dfrac{\boxed{}}{\boxed{}}$

3. Tossing a number less than 30

Chance: _____

Probability: $\dfrac{\boxed{}}{\boxed{}}$

Name_____

Writing to Explain

Which Cube? Joe and Mona each took 10 turns tossing the number cubes below. Use the results of their tosses to predict which of the two number cubes below they most likely used. Explain how you made your prediction.

Number Cube A: 2, 4, 7, 13, 16, 21   Number Cube B: 6, 12, 16, 24, 30, 31

Results of Number Cube Experiment

Name	Times even number was tossed	Times odd number was tossed
Joe	9	1
Mona	8	2

Writing a Math Explanation

- State your prediction.

- Use information from the problem to help explain your prediction.

- When a problem has choices for the answer, explain why some of the answers are not chosen.

- Use specific examples or numbers to explain why something makes sense.

Example

I think the children used *Number Cube B.*

The table tells me that most of the tosses were even numbers. *Number Cube B* has more even numbers on it than *Number Cube A.* More tosses would be even using *Number Cube B.*

---

1. Karl predicted that if he spun the spinner to the right 100 times, it would land on the letter X about the same number of times as it landed on the letter Z. Do you agree? Explain.

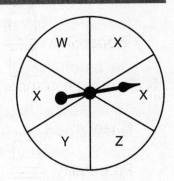

_____

_____

_____

Name_____

Mr. Tomato Juice

Donato runs a small factory that makes tomato juice. He
sells the tomato juice in 5 gal containers. How many quarts
are in 5 gal?

You know that there are 4 qt in a gallon, so multiply 5 by 4 to
find the number of quarts.

$5 \times 4 = 20$, so 5 gal = 20 qt.

1. A local restaurant ordered 9 gal of tomato
   juice. How many quarts is that?   _____

2. Donato puts a very small amount of water in
   each gallon of tomato juice he makes. Would
   he put in 3 L or 3 mL?   _____

3. Each container of Donato's tomato juice
   weighs about 8 lb. How many ounces
   is that?   _____

4. To make his tomato juice, Donato first boils
   a large amount of water. About how many
   degrees Fahrenheit would the water be when
   it is boiling?   _____

5. Donato finished making a batch of tomato
   juice at 9:15 A.M. It took him 10 min to season
   the batch. Before that, he cooked and mixed
   it for 1 hr. At what time did he begin making
   the batch?   _____

6. To make a special batch of tomato juice,
   Donato adds 3 c of vegetable juice to the
   mix. How many pints of vegetable juice does
   he add?   _____